the
PRAYER
of
LOVE

DEVOTIONAL

*Daily Readings
for Living a Life of Love*

DR. MARK HANBY
and
ROGER ROTH, SR.

HOWARD BOOKS
A DIVISION OF SIMON & SCHUSTER, INC.

New York   Nashville   London   Toronto   Sydney   New Delhi

Howard Books
A Division of Simon & Schuster, Inc.
1230 Avenue of the Americas
New York, NY 10020

First Howard Books hardcover edition November 2013

HOWARD and colophon are trademarks of Simon & Schuster, Inc.

For information about special discounts for bulk purchases, please
contact Simon & Schuster Special Sales at 1-866-506-1949 or
business@simonandschuster.com.

The Simon & Schuster Speakers Bureau can bring authors to your live event.
For more information or to book an event, contact the Simon & Schuster
Speakers Bureau at 1-866-248-3049 or visit our website at
www.simonspeakers.com.

Scripture is taken from the King James Version of the Bible, which is public
domain.

Scripture quotations marked "NKJV" are taken from the New King James
Version, copyright © 1982 by Thomas Nelson, Inc. All rights reserved. Used
by permission.

Scripture quotations marked "AMP" are from the Amplified Bible, copyright
© 1954, 1958, 1962, 1964, 1965, 1987 The Lockman Foundation. Used by
permission.

Designed by Julie Schroeder

Manufactured in the United States of America

10 9 8 7 6 5 4 3 2 1

Library of Congress Cataloging-in-Publication Data

Hanby, Mark.
   The prayer of love devotional : daily readings for living a life of love /
Dr. Mark Hanby and Roger Roth, Sr.
      p.   cm.
   1. Love—Religious aspects—Christianity—Meditations. I. Title.
BV4639.H2353   2013
242'.2—dc23   2013009028

ISBN 978-1-4767-2654-0
ISBN 978-1-4767-2655-7 (ebook)

Note: The sections at the end of each message are excerpted from *The Prayer
of Love* by Dr. Mark Hanby and Roger Roth, Sr., Howard Books, 2012. Many
have been edited for this book's purposes.

CONTENTS

the

PRAYER

of

LOVE

DEVOTIONAL

LOVE WITHOUT LIMITS

———————————

THE PRAYER OF LOVE

*And this I pray, that your **love** may abound
yet more and more*

*in **knowledge** and in all **judgment**;*

*That ye may approve things that are **excellent**;*

*that ye may be **sincere** and **without offence**
till the day of Christ;*

*Being filled with the **fruits of righteousness**,
which are by Jesus Christ,*

unto the glory and praise of God.

—PHILIPPIANS 1:9–11 (EMPHASIS ADDED)

AS YOU READ THROUGH THIS devotional on "The Prayer of Love," you will discover its immense wisdom concerning love. In so doing, you will see love from a new perspective and become aware of its magnificent power to transform your life. Whether you have already experienced some of love's mysteries or are among the many who seek to discover its greater reality, this prayer will undoubtedly awaken you to new possibilities for giving and receiving love.

Our prayer is that it will allow you to shake off the encroaching tentacles of complacency and discouragement that sometimes whisper to each of us—insisting that unconditional love may be meant for others but not for ourselves. We pray that it will encourage you to realize that love without limits is available for you.

Love without limits does not just happen but is itself a result of allowing your current level of love to grow in understanding and application of principles that cause its manifestation. It requires an affectionate desire to challenge yourself to give and receive love.

To be transformed by love is not really about effort but about awareness and an openness to let love affect you and to become effective through you. To do this, you need to keep this prayer constantly before you until it becomes formed in you. To that end this devotional is a tool to help you in your pursuit of love and its many facets.

To be transformed by love is not really about effort but about awareness and an openness to let love affect you.

The intent of this devotional is to give you a useful tool for personal edification and for fostering spiritual development. When you understand the power of love and how to appropriate its wonder in your daily living, it will change your life's focus and possibility.

This is a seven-week, or forty-nine-day, devotional. Since there are seven parts to "The Prayer of Love," it allows the reader to focus on each aspect of the prayer one day each week for seven weeks. In this manner the reader will be able to apply each aspect of the prayer to his or her life in seven unique ways.

Because the order of these seven parts is significant, *The Prayer of Love Devotional* follows the same order given in the apostle Paul's prayer to the Philippians. Each week the cycle is repeated to allow systematic growth.

Sunday—Abounding Love
Monday—Knowledge

Tuesday—Judgment
Wednesday—Approving Excellence
Thursday—Sincerity
Friday—Without Offense
Saturday—Fruits of Righteousness

The list is repeated seven times—seven being the number of divine revolutions and cycles. Seven times seven equals seven weeks/forty-nine days.

The Prayer of Love Devotional is specifically arranged to help you change old habits, develop new habits, and then reinforce your new behavior. Studies have shown that repetition is important in creating and breaking habits: it takes twenty-one days to break a habit and twenty-one days to make a new habit. The last week of the devotional exemplifies the validated New Man in Christ.

Changing Habits—Twenty-one Days
Week One: Inner Evaluation
Week Two: Defining Objectives
Week Three: Commitment

Making New Habits—Twenty-one Days
Week Four: Strengthening Character

Week Five: Operating in the Supernatural
Week Six: Living Your Ideals

REINFORCING HABITS—SEVEN DAYS
Week Seven: Testimonies of a Victorious Life

Finally, the boxed excerpts are adapted from the original book, *The Prayer of Love*.

This simple prayer is a pattern for developing maturity in Christ. The seven parts listed in the apostle Paul's prayer form benchmarks to measure our ability to give, receive, and grow in love.

The Prayer of Love Devotional is an effective way to incorporate the seven principles of love into our daily lives.

CHANGING HABITS

TWENTY-ONE DAYS

THE GREATEST SECRET

And do not be conformed to this world, but be transformed by the renewing of your mind, that you may prove what is that good and acceptable and perfect will of God.

—ROMANS 12:2, NKJV

THE GREATEST STORY EVER TOLD is the story of our redemption—it's an unfolding legacy that spans generations. It is time to discover the secret element to this story that only those chosen can experience. Jesus said, "It is given unto you to know the mysteries of the kingdom of heaven, but to them it is not given" (Matthew 13:11).

What is its great mystery? The greatest secret is that the Kingdom of God *dwells within you*! God's vast wisdom, power, and love are limitless. It unfolds in you as you change—eliminating resistance and inadequate thinking to grow in the infinite perfection of God's excellence.

The living Spirit of God already dwells inside you and cannot be altered—He's the same yesterday, today, and forever. He's Almighty, All Powerful, and Eternal. God's abounding love accomplishes the perfect will of God—His love is transformational.

Transforming, or *metamorphoo*, literally means "to have a form altered." God remains the same—but you can radically change from the inside out simply by altering your thoughts. Metamorphosis is the operation of the Holy Spirit *renewing* our minds—making it possible to

> *The greatest secret is that the Kingdom of God dwells within you!*

prove or test what's good or acceptable until you reach the perfect plan that yields the best for you.

Begin now to take steps toward renewing the thoughts of your mind. If a thought of why you can't do something or why you won't succeed or if a fearful "what if" enters your mind, you must immediately take action.

How can you tap into more of His Greatness and Power? How do you sense God's Presence within you? When do you rely on the inner promptings of the Spirit to guide you? What happens when you do?

When you pray with understanding "Let my love abound," you set in motion spiritual forces that cannot be held back. Your love must abound and increase until it becomes the God kind of love.

—ADAPTED FROM *THE PRAYER OF LOVE*

FOR YOUR THOUGHTS:

KNOW THYSELF

The first reason for man's inner slavery is his ignorance, and above all, his ignorance to himself. Without self-knowledge, without understanding the workings and function of his machine, man cannot be free, he cannot govern himself; he will always remain a slave, the plaything of forces acting upon him. This is why in all ancient teachings the first demand at the beginning of the way to liberation was to "know thyself."

—GEORGE GURDJIEFF

PLATO'S WISE COUNSEL "KNOW THYSELF" was the advice given to each person who entered the ancient Greek temple at Delphi. The Greeks believed that any liberation of the body and soul first began with careful introspection. The thorough evaluation of our feelings, thoughts, and motives reveals our strengths and weaknesses.

The apostle Paul warned the young Christians at Corinth in a similar manner. He said, "Let a man examine himself" (1 Corinthians 11:28). He understood that careful examination of our true feelings and thoughts was crucial to knowing who we are.

Personal appraisal is a tool in awakening our inner consciousness. The best way to liberate yourself is to define the thoughts, ideas, and beliefs you have.

It has been said that "we live life going forward, but we understand it looking backward." Everything about your life reflects your beliefs. Your thoughts release a creative force that frees you to soar to greater heights.

"Know thyself" sets you in the right direction for reaching your destiny—you'll know what influences your actions or controls your behavior.

All of us want to be happy, but some even dare to desire fulfillment—to look past the day-to-day stuff to perceive their potential, their *destiny*. Through this devotional, you can uncover the purpose that God sealed in your soul.

Once you discover what you're uniquely put on earth to do, you'll find what gives true meaning to your life. This knowledge becomes a tool for your personal transformation.

> *The best way to liberate yourself is to define the thoughts, ideas, and beliefs you have.*

Have you examined your true feelings and thoughts? How do you sense God influencing you? How does it give you an understanding of the meaning or purpose of your life?

When you pray, "Let my love abound," you are activating a spiritual force that will lead you to your divine image and destiny. You access divine knowledge of who you are and what is unique about you in the eyes of God.

—ADAPTED FROM *THE PRAYER OF LOVE*

FOR YOUR THOUGHTS:

A GODLY SELF-IMAGE

If there is one word which ably describes adolescence, that word is confusion. And the confusion is so strongly felt that it can easily impinge on your basic self-image. It's a sorry picture: small . . . helpless . . . powerless . . . dirty . . . socially unacceptable . . . inferior . . . confused—and in particularly bad cases, unloved and unwanted as well. And sorry though it is, the image was largely accurate when it was laid down—not by yourself, but by the actions and opinions of others. And at this stage, nature played you the dirtiest trick imaginable. You grew up, but your self-image didn't. No wonder there are so many people who aren't achieving what they would like in their lives!

—J. H. BRENNAN

RESEARCHERS AGREE THAT BY THE AGE of fourteen, 98 percent of us have a negative self-image. Deep down many of us adults still see ourselves through that initial keyhole. And because that image was almost primal in nature, regardless of what we become in life, we'll always revert to this image as "the real me" . . . unless we take action.

There's really only one way for us to grow up emotionally. We let our hearts heal—not with bandages, but rather we stitch them back together with God's truth. He's the only One we can trust to make it all right again. He tips the scales in our favor so that for once in our lives we truly feel balanced.

If we want to grow in judgment, the negative self-image has to stop. Make the decision to take responsibility for how you see yourself. From this day on, commit to view yourself as God sees you.

God tips the scales in our favor so that for once in our lives we truly feel balanced.

David said, "How precious also are thy thoughts unto me, O God! how great is the sum of them!" (Psalm 139:17). David chose to believe God. He marveled at the "sum of them"—the plans God had for him.

Let the still-small voice of who you really are grow in you. Begin to see yourself anew in the radiant Light of God's thoughts toward you. Today you can create a juncture—a moment in time that changes your life forever.

List what God has spoken specifically, in your dreams or through other people, to you about yourself. What are the messages that really excite you? How will this make a difference in the way you see yourself?

Judgment allows you to determine the proper direction of your life. Proper judgment allows you to grow in love (your perspective of God) and knowledge (your perspective of yourself— who you are and why you're here).

—ADAPTED FROM *THE PRAYER OF LOVE*

FOR YOUR THOUGHTS:

CHANGE YOUR ROUTINE

The greatest trouble with most of us is that our demands upon ourselves are so feeble, the call upon the great within us so weak and intermittent that it makes no impression upon the creative energies; it lacks the force that transmutes desires into realities.

—ORISON SWETT MARDEN

For what I am doing, I do not understand. For what I will to do, that I do not practice; but what I hate, that I do.

—ROMANS 7:15, NKJV

THE APOSTLE PAUL ASKED, "What am I doing? Why can't I stop doing it?" Sometimes we can change what we do by making better choices. But the things that are really difficult to change are those well-developed habits we do without thinking. We need an extreme makeover to force us to consciously *retrain* so we can accomplish what we plan to do.

The best way to break a bad habit is to change your routine.

How do we break bad habits? The very fact that a method or activity is a habit means we're not consciously aware of doing it. Repetition has programmed us to perform a behavioral response subconsciously. But we can develop a new program of behavior or a better response if we practice repeating it until we do it without thinking—undoing a bad habit by creating a new one.

In Philippians 3:13 we see that the apostle Paul learned to focus: "this one thing I do." He *practiced repeating* the one thing until the one thing was exactly what he wanted to do. "Forgetting those things which are behind"—it didn't matter how many years or how many failed attempts, Paul continued pressing toward the goal he wanted to achieve. We can do the same thing.

The best way to break a bad habit is to *change your rou-*

tine. In the Old Testament God had the Jews come to Jerusalem three times a year. They would stay for a week to ten days—long enough to cause them to think about what they were doing—and then return home. Consciously altering our routine affects everything else—we think about what to do next.

God is able to make all things as new in you. Do you have a habit you want to change? What will you use to replace the habit? How will you remember to do it? Create a plan.

Approving excellence is proving in yourself the value and effectiveness of allowing excellent things to change and shape your attitude and actions. Only when you have approved excellence are you able to properly deal with character traits that hinder excellence and, thus, limit love.

—ADAPTED FROM *THE PRAYER OF LOVE*

FOR YOUR THOUGHTS:

WEEK 1: INNER EVALUATION

DAY 5: SINCERITY

_____

THE CHANGE TRIGGER

_____

Are you unmindful or actually ignorant [of the fact] that
God's kindness is intended to lead you to repent—to change
your mind and inner man to accept God's will?

—ROMANS 2:4, AMP

"THE GOODNESS OF GOD LEADS you to repentance" (Romans 2:4, NKJV). Repentance is a change of mind. That's why God doesn't condemn us or make us feel guilty. He wants to lead us into something much better for us.

God makes it so easy for us. He gives us the opportunity to change simply by thinking His wonderful thoughts. If we think His thoughts often enough, we not only change the way we think, we become who we are meant to be— gifted, talented, successful, determined, confident, lovable, and sincere.

We are what we think. Solomon said, "For as he thinketh in his heart, so is he" (Proverbs 23:7). Repentance is as easy as thinking better thoughts—God's thoughts for us. When we do this, we start accepting God's will for us.

If this change of thought is maintained, true liberation influences our decisions and experiences. Thinking beyond our limitations will shift us into a state of true happiness.

We show signs of growth when we let go of long-held resentments. And changing thoughts to expectations is a sure sign of spiritual growth.

Henry David Thoreau believed, "We must learn to reawaken and keep ourselves awake, not by mechanical aids, but by an infinite expectation of the dawn." What do we expect? *Questions* open us to expectancy—we expect answers. If we question our purpose, it will trigger a new awareness for solutions and opportunities.

The "expectation of the dawn" that Thoreau spoke of refers to our *expecting* to see God's hand awakening our purpose. We can raise expectations when we "treat people as if they were what they ought to be and . . . help them to

Repentance is as easy as thinking better thoughts.

become what they are capable of being" (Johann Wolfgang von Goethe).

Change first starts in our thoughts—our thoughts set us free. What can you do to change your thoughts? What could you listen to or read that might trigger a good change in you? What would be an awakening "by an infinite expectation of the dawn" in your life?

Though we often try to escape from unpleasant thoughts, our minds have no off-buttons.

—ADAPTED FROM *THE PRAYER OF LOVE*

FOR YOUR THOUGHTS:

THE BREAKTHROUGH
OF FORGIVENESS

---

*Put off the old man . . . Put on the new man who
is renewed in knowledge according to the
image of Him who created him.*

—COLOSSIANS 3:9–10, NKJV

MOST OF US HAVE NEGATIVE pictures that flash through our minds from time to time. These negative images or memories result from old thought habits. They may seem to occur spontaneously, from nowhere—but they don't.

Every imagination is the result of some belief we had some time in our lives. If we see an image of failure or have a feeling of doom, it's springing from some belief we buried deep within. If we were hurt in the past, that feeling may cause us to fear that it's happening again. This feeling is negative visualization. If we allow it to continue instead of stopping it immediately, it will make change difficult.

Our feelings are true; we may have been hurt. The damage is that we equate every situation with that feeling, and it's not the truth *now*.

One way we can create a breakthrough is through forgiveness. When we forgive the trespasser for what happened in the past, we can stop carrying the bondage of our past into another day—a bondage that limits our present possibility so we can start living as the New Man in Christ today.

Another way we create a breakthrough is taking control of offensive thoughts. And we *can* control our thoughts.

Forgiveness creates a breakthrough in our lives that allows us to start living as the New Man in Christ today.

Being a New Man in Christ means replacing the old memory with a new action of belief. If some negative image or thought flashes into your mind, forcefully say, "*Stop!*" Then affirm, "I'm the redeemed of the Lord—only God's truth dwells in my mind now!"

Even if we can't feel justified in forgiving our offender, we can lift our thoughts "to the Rock that is higher" than we are— as the old hymn says—and believe that God's truth and mercy include total forgiveness.

> *Being a New Man in Christ means replacing the old memory with a new action of belief.*

What thoughts can we control? How will we speak the truth over this memory of pain or lies? Have you had a breakthrough moment? Have you forgiven? If not, why? Why would you want to resist change if it's destroying your future growth and success? Are you willing to step on God's rock of truth and mercy by saying, "I forgive because God forgave them"?

The whole world is offended. People are hurt. But the antidote to being offended is forgiving.

—ADAPTED FROM *THE PRAYER OF LOVE*

FOR YOUR THOUGHTS:

WE SHALL NOT BE MOVED

He will not suffer thy foot to be moved: he that keepeth thee will not slumber. . . . The Lord is thy keeper: the Lord is thy shade upon thy right hand. . . . The Lord shall preserve thee from all evil: he shall preserve thy soul. The Lord shall preserve thy going out and thy coming in from this time forth, and even for evermore.

—PSALM 121:3, 5, 7–8

THE PROMISE OF GOD KEEPS us from falling. We stand on a firm foundation—we shall not be moved. God wrote Truth on our hearts and set us as pillars in His sanctuary.

God keeps us by His Power, preserves us by His Grace, and guides us by His Counsel. The Watchful Keeper will never slumber for a moment—He always looks upon us, so we are safe. God promised the Hebrews that they would not disappear from the face of the earth—four thousand years later His declaration still holds true and Israel remains the apple of His eye.

The "shade" the psalmist mentions refers to protection or defense—God set a pillar of fire to protect in the night and a pillar cloud to protect in the day. He set His Spirit as Watchman and Keeper of our souls. God is able to keep all that is entrusted into His care (see 2 Timothy 1:12).

God keeps us by His Power, preserves us by His Grace, and guides us by His Counsel.

God promised us that He will work everything together for our good. The negative effect of sin is overcome by the power of His grace. All souls are His—no one can take us out of His hand. No purpose of God can be withheld from Him.

The God who keeps our feet from slipping also promised to prosper us wherever we go (see Genesis 28:14–15)—in the words we speak, in the workplace, in the relationships we enter, in the decisions we make, and in the coming and going of ministry in His Presence.

God upholds His people today and "for evermore." The vast gulf of time is governed by His laws. All who follow Him are safe.

Do you walk in the freedom of being totally protected? If so, in what areas? How can you allow for this freedom to be further developed in your life?

Righteousness exalts a person, a family, or a nation.

—ADAPTED FROM *THE PRAYER OF LOVE*

FOR YOUR THOUGHTS:

ALL YOU NEED

Love is the only creative, redemptive,
transforming power in the universe.

—MARTIN LUTHER KING, JR.

LOVE CHANGES THE WAY WE think, speak, and behave. Love impacts everything. It activates the inexhaustible power of God that transforms us—allowing access to a life of abundance.

"For God so loved the world that He gave His only begotten Son, that whoever believes in Him should not perish but have everlasting life" (John 3:16, NKJV). God loved His creation through His Son. Jesus is the expression of who God is in a bodily form that can be understood by everyone.

Love's highest expression is found in our desire for another's good.

Love is a universal language. It's an emotion that is comprehensible, and it not only stirs man's heart but also empowers him to do great exploits for those he loves. John Lennon summed it up with the lyric "All you need is love."

Everything we experience is due to the law of our minds. As the nineteenth-century philosopher and psychologist William James said, "Belief creates the actual fact." James discovered that "by changing [our] inner attitudes of mind, [we] can change the outer aspects of [our] lives." Thoughts create. Thoughts are things. What we feel strongly about we'll attract to us and what we imagine about ourselves we'll become.

We cannot think evil and reap good or think good and reap evil. That's why negative thoughts generated toward others will eventually destroy us. But positive thoughts always benefit everyone—they are a blessing.

God's love is a force that flows through us just as our blood flows through our veins. His love surging through us to others has the added benefit of energizing every cell in our bodies. That means if we pray and desire others to be successful, happy, and enhanced in every good thing, we receive the same benefits. Love's highest expression is found in our desire for another's good—it opens the storehouses of God.

Jesus had compassion for the sick and healed them. Compassion is the activation of our power to love. Love is the way to higher awareness—because we love, we see what else we can do.

Do you take time each day to pray for God's blessing and goodness on your family and friends? How does God love others through you? How do you feel godly compassion?

There is a language of the Spirit, and it is the communication of love.

—ADAPTED FROM *THE PRAYER OF LOVE*

FOR YOUR THOUGHTS:

CONCENTRATION OF POWER

---

*Multitudes of people, drifting aimlessly to and fro without
a set purpose, deny themselves such fulfillment of their
capacities, and the satisfying happiness which attends it. . . .
As we harness our abilities to a steady purpose and undertake
the long pull toward its accomplishment, rich compensations
reward us. A sense of purpose simplifies life and therefore
concentrates our abilities; and concentration adds power.*

—KENNETH HILDEBRAND

*Brethren, I count not myself to have apprehended: but this
one thing I do, forgetting those things which are behind,
and reaching forward unto those things which are before,
I press toward the mark for the prize of the
high calling of God in Christ Jesus.*

—PHILIPPIANS 3:13–14

"ONE THING I DO" was the apostle Paul's step into prosperity. He narrowed his focus to one area. He concentrated on his goal. And he knew how to be more productive in reaching it. He had a plan: purge his mind of past failures and direct all his thoughts to one thing—

Our purpose is closely related to what stirs our hearts.

his goal. His thoughts became a powerful, creative force in manifesting purpose. Paul knew the truth about himself—he knew God's will and it gave him purpose.

Hildebrand further defined those without purpose: "They are not wicked; they are only shallow. They are not mean or vicious; they simply are empty. . . . They lack range, depth, and conviction. Without purpose their lives ultimately wander into the morass of dissatisfaction." They are aimless, directionless, meaningless, pointless, useless—purposeless.

Our purpose is closely related to what stirs our hearts. David prophesied of Jesus saying, "Zeal for Your house has eaten me up" (Psalm 69:9, NKJV). Jesus desired to fulfill His purpose—it consumed His thoughts, fueled His passion for the lost, and it moved Him with compassion to heal the sick, raise the dead, feed the multitudes.

What do you love to do—what means a lot to you? Is there a Scripture or a quote that defines it? How can you

rearrange your daily itinerary to concentrate more on fulfilling your purpose? Are there goals to reach? What one
thing can you do today to bring you closer to accomplish-
ing your goal?

Love lays down its life. Love gives, fear withholds. Love sur-
renders, fear threatens. If you truly love, then you are willing
not just to give things, but willing to give yourself.

—ADAPTED FROM *THE PRAYER OF LOVE*

FOR YOUR THOUGHTS:

WEEK 2: DEFINING OBJECTIVES
DAY 10: JUDGMENT

———

KINGDOM FITNESS

———

No man, having put his hand to the plough, and looking
back, is fit for the kingdom of God.

—LUKE 9:62

Fortunate is the person who has developed the self-control
to steer a straight course toward his objective in life,
without being swayed from his purpose by either
commendation or condemnation.

—NAPOLEON HILL

JESUS ILLUSTRATED THE KEY ELEMENT for success: keep your eyes focused on what's ahead of you, on what's possible. Once you make a decision, once you start walking forward, never stop and second-guess your efforts. After determining a plan of action, you'll become more decisive in your approach if you forget what's behind and continue with your plan.

We lose our chance to grow in love if we continually check our effectiveness through what we've accomplished, regret what we started, or ask, "Am I good enough?" Those mighty in His Kingdom developed a plan and then followed it. They became interested in where they were going, not in comparing themselves to others.

Kingdom fitness requires discipline to make it effective. Whatever we choose to do, we must hold ourselves to the course we set—we're disciplined. The "field" is the area we choose to discipline. We grip the "plough" and move forward, determined to finish well. We train ourselves to make good choices by using what's in our hands—within our God-given ability and power.

Some of us failed in the past because we couldn't remain determined. Today let us finish our course. Write down what you expect to plow and the direction you'll take—and refuse to falter or turn back.

God uses the little things we do every day to make us diligent. If we are disciplined to accomplish the smaller tasks, we are given more authority and rule. Put your hand to the plow, and control or govern yourself to rule over it.

Benjamin Franklin said, "He is a governor that governs his passions, and he is a servant that serves them." Are you a governor or a servant? Do you discipline yourself to rule over your passions? What passions do you want to rule over instead of serve? How do you prepare to be fit for the Kingdom?

> *Whatever we choose to do, we must hold ourselves to the course we set.*

Judgment is simply the ability to make a proper decision between two things. When you make judgments, you make a decision to do something or not to do it; to accept or to reject; to do good or to do evil; to help or to withhold help; to love or to hold back love; to seek your divine connection or to remain as you are.

—ADAPTED FROM *THE PRAYER OF LOVE*

FOR YOUR THOUGHTS:

WEEK 2: DEFINING OBJECTIVES

DAY 11: APPROVING EXCELLENCE

———————

A Time for
Every Purpose

———————

*To every thing there is a season, and a time to
every purpose under the heaven.*

—ECCLESIASTES 3:1

HOW EMPOWERING IT IS TO know that the events happening in life are ordained of God—that no purpose of God is withheld from us (Job 42:2). But it is also true that there is a time to *participate* with God in walking out our dreams and goals.

We all greet each new day with the same twenty-four hours to fulfill our responsibilities and obligations—time for eating and sleeping, for relaxing and celebrating. Everyone has at least a moment each day to do exactly what he or she wants—even if it's only to visualize it.

Take inventory of a typical day. Set up the day like an itinerary. There will always be days when the children are sick or tragedy strikes, but most days we sleep, work, eat, and relax with some type of recreation or hobby.

One of the best suggestions I ever received was not to waste my time on useless pursuits. *Useless*—if it's not productive or worthwhile, it's a waste of time. You can ask objectively: What did I learn yesterday? Did I have a schedule that I followed? Did I make a difference in someone's life?

Success is planned. You can plan to add importance to your life. If you don't have time during your day, why not get up fifteen minutes earlier? What if you watched TV for only half the time or for just one program? Would that give you more time for working toward your goal—becoming more aware of what else you could do with your time or with the plan for reaching your goals?

To wisely utilize your time, you need a schedule. What would be your ideal schedule if you had all the time you needed? What can you add or change in your daily routine that would incorporate your ideal use of time? Can you add fifteen minutes or even an hour a day for doing something productive or fun?

_____

You can plan to add importance to your life.

_____

What would happen if you added doing things you like to your schedule for a week? You'd be well on your way to making it a habit. Take some time now to write a schedule you can live your life by—or make it your plan to do one thing differently each day until you are living your ideal life.

The greatest spiritual achievers may seldom come up on the radar screen of the world's most famous and influential people, but if they have learned how to find and walk toward their destiny, their impact upon eternal things is as great as any.

—ADAPTED FROM *THE PRAYER OF LOVE*

FOR YOUR THOUGHTS:

SPECIAL IDENTITY

---

*Now therefore, if you will indeed obey My voice and
keep My covenant, then you shall be a special treasure to
Me above all people; for all the earth is Mine.*

—EXODUS 19:5, NKJV

*What lies behind us and what lies before us are tiny
matters, compared to what lies within us.*

—RALPH WALDO EMERSON

"LET US MAKE MAN IN our image" (Genesis 1:26) are priceless words. God defines our unequivocal value and worth to Him then . . . now . . . and forevermore. Our value is that we are made in the image of God—we're spiritual beings.

When in Exodus 19:5 God calls us "peculiar," meaning special, He stresses our having the same identity, character, and purpose that He has. "Special treasure" means we have His essence manifesting in us as Christ—meaning we become the express image of His purpose. It's important to know our identity is in Christ and not in what we do.

Identity is everything. It takes far more work to change a misguided identity than it does to change a corrupt attitude, behavior, or purpose. That's why God started with identity—He defined who we are in Him first by showing us who He is.

God didn't create you as average but as special and powerful. No one else will ever compare to you.

God made mankind in His image, to bear His likeness. God didn't create you as average but as special and powerful. No one else will ever compare to you.

Your sincerity manifests through aligning to His eternal truth and love. If you are attuned to the voice of God within, you will hold on to what He reveals by taking it seriously. You will believe it's true and act accordingly.

Did you know that you reveal just how powerful God is to you by your willingness to receive what He says about you? What will you draw from His vast richness of power?

God cannot lie. He means what He says. When God says, "You are Mine," do you believe it? How much are you willing to receive from God—how much do you believe He's capable of delivering to you?

We should try in everything we do to make sure that our yes is yes and our no is no. In other words we should say what we mean and mean what we say, and be willing to stand by our words.

—ADAPTED FROM *THE PRAYER OF LOVE*

FOR YOUR THOUGHTS:

CAUGHT IN A LOOP

---

*Perfectionism is a refusal to let yourself move ahead. It is a
loop—an obsessive, debilitating closed system that causes
you to get stuck in the details of what you are writing or
painting or making and to lose sight of the whole.
Instead of creating freely and allowing errors
to reveal themselves later as insights, we often
get mired in getting the details right.*

—JULIA CAMERON

REMEMBER VINYL PHONOGRAPH RECORDS? A scratched record made the needle stick rather than move smoothly forward. The needle literally stuck in a crevice and played the same words and notes over and over without any hope of changing—unless there was outside intervention.

In opening your soul to opportunity, you come face-to-face with God's purpose.

The children of Israel were mentally stuck in a rut and couldn't move forward into the Promised Land. They would have died in the wilderness if Moses hadn't interceded for them. God said, "You have circled this mountain long enough; turn northward."

Most people aren't even aware that their thoughts keep circling the same well-worn grooves. When they were hurt, they found safety in a foxhole—they just never came out. Now they're stagnating in a rut and too offended to step out. Examples of rut thinking:

1. We are victims held hostage. We blame someone else for our circumstances—thinking there's nothing we can do.

2. We are overwhelmed. We have too much to do. So we quit trying to catch up.

3. We are perfectionists. We get stuck reworking the

details and never move forward; or else we won't do anything unless we can do it perfectly the first time.

4. We live in paralyzing fear of failure or criticism. We're sure we will never be good enough or smart enough, so we do nothing.

There are ways that God triggers change in your life. Many times He simply paints a picture of your true identity to inspire or motivate a deeper desire to take the necessary steps into your future. In opening your soul to opportunity, you come face-to-face with God's purpose.

Ruts are never easy to confront. Yet if you take that first step, you may find a vista of opportunity. Are there any hurts/offenses/ruts in your life? Can they be breached with forgiveness? How can you step into a brighter path?

Offense is a crippler even if the cause of the offense is 100 percent the fault of another person. We might feel justified in being offended, but it will never provide mental or emotional liberty.

—ADAPTED FROM *THE PRAYER OF LOVE*

FOR YOUR THOUGHTS:

WEEK 2: DEFINING OBJECTIVES

DAY 14: FRUITS OF RIGHTEOUSNESS

DUNAMIS POWER

Genius is present in every age, but the men carrying it within them remain benumbed unless extraordinary events occur to heat up and melt the mass so that it flows forth.

—DENIS DIDEROT

But we have this treasure in earthen vessels, that the excellency of the power may be of God, and not of us.

—2 CORINTHIANS 4:7

THE EARTH'S CRUST IS EIGHTEEN miles deep. It seems like a thick crust—yet in perspective it's thinner than the ratio of an eggshell to its yolk. Mankind sits on top of a thin crust, but hidden beneath it is enough fervent heat to melt diamonds.

Occasionally the great pressure of this huge inner force causes a shift in land plates and molten lava erupts through small gaps or crevices in the crust. The eruption causes gold, diamonds, and silver to form in places that later can be handled or mined.

God chose to release His power through earthen vessels. He sealed the essence of His spirituality in us. In Greek, *dunamis* is defined as "force, miraculous power, ability, abundance, meaning, working of miracles"—it's His resurrection power in us. That means there's a vast amount of unstoppable power ready to break free within us.

The treasure is the excellence of His power. Sometimes God uses events to shift our plane of thought—using trials and experiences to force a change in our perception. It allows gold, diamonds, silver, precious stones to surface. Those who discern the supernatural realm can actually see precious stones in our auras, thoughts, and speech.

Your fruits of righteousness are the product of spiritual matter that forced a break through your outer shell of defense. Why wait for a volcanic eruption to release His treasure? Sometimes it's as simple as a twinkle in the eye, brimming tears, a sweet sigh, a handshake, a heartfelt smile, or the words you speak. It's how God loves the world through you.

There's a vast amount of unstoppable power ready to break free within us.

What's formed in our thoughts and emotions can also be released through our creative expressions: music, art, science, literature, craftsmanship, cooking. We all have *dunamis* power within us—it's how we express it that makes us unique. What is your talent, gifting, ability?

How you tend what is given to you by God will determine the quality and quantity of your fruit. Becoming fruitful is not so much about the fruit as it is about your ability to produce fruit. Spiritual maturity gives you that ability.

—ADAPTED FROM *THE PRAYER OF LOVE*

FOR YOUR THOUGHTS:

———————

Unlocking
Your Potential

———————

*Then said Jesus said to those Jews which believed on
him, If ye continue in my word, then are ye my
disciples indeed; And ye shall know the truth,
and the truth shall make you free.*

—JOHN 8:31–32

GOD IS LOVE. IF YOU choose to walk in love, then you walk in His Word. Freedom comes from being disciplined to walk in love.

If you discipline yourself to walk in love, you free yourself from everything that once held you in bondage, weakness, or indecisiveness. Winston Churchill noted, "Continuous effort, not strength or intelligence, is the key to unlocking our potential."

Scottish essayist Thomas Carlyle said, "There must be a beginning to any great matter, but the continuing to the end until it be thoroughly finished yields the true glory." Those who discipline themselves to persevere until the task is completed reach their full potential—they reach their destiny.

Whatever you choose to accomplish, you must be disciplined to do it. This is one of the greatest lessons you can learn because it's the basis of any future growth.

Those who discipline themselves to persevere until the task is completed reach their full potential.

If you discipline yourself to live a life of love, love will overflow to all you come in contact with. If you discipline yourself to live as Christ lived, you bear the fruit of His anointing. He promises you, "Herein is my Father glorified, that ye bear much fruit; so shall ye be my disciples" (John 15:8). Disciples choose to live like Christ; therefore they prosper.

Anyone can do something once, but it takes perseverance to make it a lifestyle. Aristotle said, "I count him braver who overcomes his desires than him who conquers his enemies; for the hardest victory is over self." The difficulty is doing it all the time—regardless of whether you feel like it or not.

Are you disciplined? If you plan to do something, do you accomplish it? In what areas do you lack discipline? What can you do to become more consistent in your walk with God?

God is love. That is His essence. To live a life rooted in love is to fulfill His Commandments. Your ultimate purpose is to discover, to express, and to be ruled by love.

—ADAPTED FROM *THE PRAYER OF LOVE*

FOR YOUR THOUGHTS:

BENEFIT OF THE DOUBT

----

*Perhaps the greatest charity comes when we are kind
to each other, when we don't judge or categorize
someone else, when we simply give each other
the benefit of the doubt or remain quiet.*

—MARVIN J. ASHTON

GOD GAVE THE APOSTLE PETER a vision of unclean animals in a sheet coming down from heaven. A voice said that God had now declared them clean. The Spirit then told Peter about the men at the door asking for him, saying, "Go with them, doubting nothing" (Acts 10:20).

Peter didn't understand what the vision meant. He had to make a choice. Why is it so easy to dismiss something and say it can't be of God? Perhaps he wondered, *Why would God show me this?* God asked Peter to give Him the benefit of the doubt.

Giving God the benefit of the doubt means the situation could go either way. We don't know—so why not trust that it really is of God?

Often our conscious or objective mind will fight against our subconscious—the inner knowledge gained through the Spirit. If we give God the benefit of the doubt, we'll learn to discern His voice. Looking for direction and guidance develops our ability to hear through our Christ-consciousness.

Every time you respond to a prompting you feel is from God, you are using and strengthening your spiritual receptors. It's time to develop an ability to perceive God by commanding your inner man to be aware of any change—

gut feelings, visions, sounds, scents. How you sense God may be different from the way someone else does.

Spiritual triggers alert us the same way motion detectors or fire alarms do. They catch our attention, perhaps to warn us or to give us a flash of insight that speaks of possibility. We decide

If we give God the benefit of the doubt, we'll learn to discern His voice.

how to respond and then practice until we know when our subconscious intuition is alerting us in every situation.

How do you decide if something is of God or not? How do you give God the benefit of the doubt? What's the worst that could happen if something wasn't of God?

Love will make me hope for the best and give others the benefit of the doubt.

—ADAPTED FROM *THE PRAYER OF LOVE*

FOR YOUR THOUGHTS:

WEEK 3: COMMITMENT

DAY 17: JUDGMENT

Re-create Your Mind

For the word of God is quick, and powerful, and sharper than any twoedged sword, piercing even to the dividing asunder of soul and spirit, and of the joints and marrow, and is a discerner of the thoughts and intents of the heart.

—HEBREWS 4:12

THE THINGS THAT COME OUT of the heart have a tremendous influence over our minds and affect every decision we make. We may feel an inner knowing or a small voice urging us to do something. The Spirit of God communes with us and prompts us by influencing our emotions and thoughts.

Animals innately know how to survive without instruction or hesitation—their instincts fashion their behavior. Man has similar instincts. No one teaches a baby to suck and to crawl; no one tells our hearts to beat and our eyes to blink.

Your subconscious mind governs your vital organs and keeps you internally balanced. But you can consciously interfere with its performance by thinking negatively, allowing things such as worry or angry thoughts to dominate your mind. Negativity upsets the divine balance programmed for your body.

The apostle Paul said, "Be renewed in the spirit of your mind" (Ephesians 4:23). You can change from just existing to walking purposefully by examining what you do. It's a judgment call—you decide if your actions are agreeable with your spirit. Do they benefit others?

The Word of God is your constant guide and counselor. Meditating on or memorizing the Word of God will re-create your subconscious into the mind of Christ. If you program your subconscious mind with the truth, you'll immediately recognize the promptings and admonitions of God.

We all need time to re-create our minds. Some activities rest your mind, emptying it of all the clutter accumulated during the busy day or week. When you bring harmony and balance back into

You can change from just existing to walking purposefully by examining what you do.

play, you can refocus on what's important. Do something that purges your mind. Find what works for you and schedule time to re-create your mind—and touch base with your divinity.

Judgment is the ability to make good choices in your life, because you realize you are part of God's universe, part of a greater plan.

—ADAPTED FROM *THE PRAYER OF LOVE*

FOR YOUR THOUGHTS:

THE MOMENT WE COMMIT

Until one is committed, there is hesitancy, the chance to draw back, always ineffectiveness. Concerning all acts of initiative (and creation), there is one elementary truth, the ignorance of which kills countless ideas and splendid plans: that the moment one definitely commits oneself, then Providence moves too. A whole stream of events issues from the decision, raising in one's favor all manner of unforeseen incidents, meetings and material assistance, which no man could have dreamt would have come his way.

—W. H. MURRAY

A RE YOU COMMITTED TO EXCELLENCE? Are you determined to finish the course you started? This is an exercise in follow-through. If you are totally committed, you can change your life. Are you willing to carry out a specific plan, bring the idea into fruition?

If you answered, "Yes!" then expect God to be working in you to fulfill your goal in an excellent manner. The moment you commit is the moment you start seeing the hand of God in operation in your life. "With God all things are possible" (Matthew 19:26).

"Now unto him that is able to do exceeding abundantly above all that we ask or think, according to the power that worketh in us" (Ephesians 3:20). *Worketh* in the Greek language means "to energize, operate, empower, motivate, and impassion."

God's miraculous power works in us and unfolds the ability or intelligence we need to do extraordinary things. It's thrilling when an idea or plan comes to us. But sometimes we fail by not following through.

The moment you commit is the moment you start seeing the hand of God in operation in your life.

The difference between *wishing* and *planning* will always be found in our personal commitment. Commitment develops a disciplined, persistent, and determined character. It's God working in us to accomplish His plans.

You can create a great follow-through pattern in your life—a pattern that leads to excellence. Are you decisive? Once you make a decision, do you carry it out? Are you often tempted to second-guess or overrule it? How can you be better equipped to be committed? Is there a Scripture that can strengthen you in your decision?

The moment of empowerment is now, the present. It is not lost in your past failures or a moment to be reached in your future—your empowerment is always in the present moment. Therefore the convergence of possibility opens new doors for you, and a brand-new beginning—now.

—ADAPTED FROM *THE PRAYER OF LOVE*

FOR YOUR THOUGHTS:

WEEK 3: COMMITMENT

DAY 19: SINCERITY

———————

THE GREATER LAW

———————

Verily, verily, I say unto you, I am the door of the sheep.
All that ever came before me are thieves and robbers:
but the sheep did not hear them. I am the door: by me if
any man enter in, he shall be saved, and shall go
in and out, and find pasture. The thief cometh not,
but for to steal, and to kill, and to destroy: I am come
that they might have life, and that they might have it more
abundantly. I am the good shepherd: the good
shepherd giveth his life for the sheep.

—JOHN 10:7–11

WHAT DO WE CONSIDER a more abundant life to be? Do we think it can be experienced financially as well as spiritually? What about creative expression? Do we dare believe His Word is sincere—that He really means for us to prosper and abound in all areas of our lives? If we don't believe God is sincere, it will make it difficult for us to grow in sincerity.

> *To activate the blessing, you must believe it is for you.*

Does God want to bless us? How we respond indicates how we view ourselves. Every thought is an image of something we believe is true about us—negative or positive. Memories from our pasts cause us to think or feel this way about ourselves.

One way to enhance or replace a memory is to commit to memorizing Scripture. God's Word has power over all our fears—He's Almighty. What He says happens. "I am come that they might have life, and that they might have it more abundantly" (John 10:10). Anything in our life can change if we replace it with His greater law, but to activate the blessing, you must believe it is for you—exposing the measure of your sincerity.

Maybe the real thief stealing our promise for more abundance is our lack of trust that God means to bless us *individually.* Think of the joy our lives would reflect if we believed God predestined us to be blessed more abundantly. What other Scriptures would bless us if we believed God intended them for us when He spoke them?

Do you really believe that Jesus came to give you life more abundantly? If you believe you were His intention, make a short-range goal along with a plan to achieve it. What would you like to have accomplished by the end of the forty-nine days?

You are not pressured to be something different than you are. Instead you are confident and at peace because you understand who you are and what you are destined to do in God's purpose.

—ADAPTED FROM *THE PRAYER OF LOVE*

FOR YOUR THOUGHTS:

WEEK 3: COMMITMENT

DAY 20: WITHOUT OFFENSE

My Soul Waits

---

*Behold, I go forward, but he is not there; and
backward, but I cannot perceive him: On the left hand,
where he doth work, but I cannot behold him:
he hideth himself on the right hand, that I cannot see
him: But he knoweth the way that I take: when he
hath tried me, I shall come forth as gold.*

—JOB 23:8–10

SOMETIMES LIFE THROWS A BLOW that shakes our souls. We're devastated. Our minds are full of big questions: *What did I do wrong? Did God forsake me? Why didn't I see it coming?*

When Job was confused, he stopped. Job couldn't find God, so he waited until God found him. Likewise, we must wait on God. When what we sensed as His will proves not to be, we often don't know what to do. It's best just to stop looking for a way out with our plan B, and quiet our souls with the knowledge that God knows where we are even if we can't see Him.

David said in Psalms 139:1–5:

O Lord, thou hast searched me, and known me. Thou knowest my downsitting and mine uprising, thou understandest my thought afar off. Thou compassest my path and my lying down, and art acquainted with all my ways. For there is not a word in my tongue, but, lo, O LORD, thou knowest it altogether. Thou hast beset me behind and before, and laid thine hand upon me.

God knows our lifestyle, our thoughts, and our habits— God knows when even a hair falls from our heads. God works everything together *for good*—even when we don't understand at the moment.

When King David's faith was shaken, he wrote, "Truly my soul silently waits for God; from Him comes my salvation. He only *is* my rock and my salvation; He is my defense; I shall not be greatly moved" (Psalm 62:1–2, NKJV). David did not become offended and blame God for what happened to him or for not helping him sooner. He had confidence in God.

> *God works everything together for good—even when we don't understand at the moment.*

Confidence means to be "with faith." Our faith is in the God who dwells within us. Citing His Word strengthens us: "For he hath said, I will never leave thee, nor forsake thee" (Hebrews 13:5). "If God be for us, who can be against us?" (Romans 8:31). "For with God nothing shall be impossible" (Luke 1:37). As our thoughts rest on God, our confidence renews.

Has your faith ever been shaken? Did you blame God . . . yourself? What Scripture or quote encouraged you? What did you learn—how did everything work together according to His purpose?

The truth is, we live in a world where natural actions have spiritual consequences. There is a certain wobble in the spirit world just as there is in the spinning and rotation of the earth so that every few years we have a leap year. Like the leap year, every so often we should make an adjustment—find a time to judge our spiritual maturity. Maybe at those times we should go back and take a closer look at our lives and see why things are not working the way we think they should work.

—ADAPTED FROM *THE PRAYER OF LOVE*

FOR YOUR THOUGHTS:

DARE TO BE MAGNIFICENT

---

*It is our light, not our darkness, that most frightens us. We
ask ourselves, "Who am I to be brilliant, gorgeous, talented
and fabulous?" Actually, who are you not to be? You are a
child of God. Your playing small doesn't serve the world.
There's nothing enlightened about shrinking so that other
people won't feel insecure around you. . . . We are born to
make manifest the glory of God that is within us. It's not
just in some of us; it's in everyone. And as we let our own
light shine, we unconsciously give other people permission
to do the same. As we are liberated from our own fears,
our presence automatically liberates others.*

—MARIANNE WILLIAMSON

LIFE HAS GOD'S FINGERPRINTS all over it—His vibrational energy is sealed into every molecule! "All things were made through Him" (John 1:3, NKJV). We are stamped as "the express image of His person" (Hebrews 1:3, NKJV) and filled with His infinite Spirit.

If we want to discover something or someone's essence, we look at the core structure or its nature. Our essence of power is the Spirit within—He carries the same power force as the Creator. All matter takes on the essence of the Creator. The visible and invisible are made of one and the same Spirit.

The ocean and all its droplets keep the same chemical composition. Likewise a vial of our blood is identical to what's flowing in our veins. Jesus said, "I am the vine, ye are the branches" (John 15:5). We are one in Him—created in the image of our Creator. It's the same Spirit of Life abiding in Him who gives us the ability to be a vital life force in the world today.

These powerful forces are deep within you, waiting to be released. How you express the creative Spirit within you is your uniqueness. It's who you are . . . what you are meant to be.

Philosopher and physician Albert Schweitzer viewed the substance of a man's life by the Spirit of God he possessed: "Your life is something opaque, not transparent, as long as you look at it in an ordinary human way. But if you hold it up against the light of God's goodness, it shines and turns transparent, radiant and bright. And then you ask yourself in amazement: Is this really my own life I see before me?"

It's the same Spirit of Life abiding in Him who gives us the ability to be a vital life force in the world today.

What would be different if you believed God filled you with everything you need to be magnificent? What would be happening in your life? How would you express the magnificent spirit within you?

Being filled with the fruit of righteousness means I have the ability to possess fruit beyond measure.

—ADAPTED FROM *THE PRAYER OF LOVE*

FOR YOUR THOUGHTS:

MAKING NEW HABITS

TWENTY-ONE DAYS

SWEET SURRENDER

---

*Few souls understand what God would accomplish
in them if they were to abandon themselves unreservedly
to Him and if they were to allow His grace to
mold them accordingly.*

—IGNATIUS

*The reason why many are still troubled, still seeking,
still making little forward progress is because they haven't
yet come to the end of themselves. We're still trying
to give orders, and interfering with God's work within us.*

—A. W. TOZER

A MARK OF MATURITY IS our ability to surrender: to relinquish possession, power, authority or control to another.

Surrender is a response on our part—an openness or willingness to receive. The author David R. Hawkins said, "Devotion enables surrender of the mind's vanities and cherished illusions so that it progressively becomes more free and more open to the light of Truth."

Prayer is a very effective way of surrendering our will to God's.

A. W. Tozer said, "The degree of blessing enjoyed by any man will correspond exactly with the completeness of God's victory over us." Are we open to receive God's love—knowing the more we receive love, the more freedom and power we walk in?

How much you surrender will depend on the clarity of your vision. Mother Teresa had a very clear Word from God: "to love and serve the poor and to see Jesus in everyone." She surrendered to God's call on her life and left the convent to live with the poor. Her ministry grew and in the 1990s had more than one million coworkers in more than forty countries.

Prayer is a very effective way of surrendering our will to God's. It is only when God is in control and we align with

Him that we experience the power of His love flowing through us to accomplish His plan. Jesus prayed to the Father saying, "If it be possible, let this cup pass from me: nevertheless not as I will, but as thou wilt" (Matthew 26:39).

Have you abandoned your will to surrender to God's? Was love a factor in your yielding? What aligned in your life to the spiritual? What does it mean to experience real power? Did God give you a clear vision of His will in a particular area?

In many ways these benchmarks are measurements of our ability to give, receive, and grow in love. Love is the moving force of the universe. It is the force that causes all people to live rightly and to respond properly in every situation.

—ADAPTED FROM *THE PRAYER OF LOVE*

FOR YOUR THOUGHTS:

WEEK 4: STRENGTHENING CHARACTER

DAY 23: KNOWLEDGE

ETERNAL ELIXIR

---

*Faith is the "eternal elixir" which gives life, power
and action to the impulse of thought! Faith is the starting
point of all accumulation of riches! Faith is the
basis of all "miracles" and all mysteries which cannot be
analyzed by the rules of science! Faith is the
only known antidote for failure!*

—NAPOLEON HILL

SOME BLAME GOD OR OTHERS for why their lives are off track and unproductive. They feel disappointed or frustrated that things aren't the way they want them to be.

Sometimes it's merely a misdirected thought. Instead of carrying a joyous, peaceful expectation that your wants will happen, maybe you expect that what you want will never happen—and you have a list of excuses to prove it.

Thoughts create a mental block if they're made up of doubts, fears, jealousy, or selfishness. One way you can empower your thoughts is to focus on truth. If you believe God's Word is for you, you can walk in His power. The power of Love enables you to do God's will.

Christ is the light of the world—Christ consciousness is a state where we recognize that Light. The greater work of our soul is to lift our thoughts to such heights in Christ that we comprehend and manifest the greatness of God.

The power of Love enables you to do God's will.

Your Christ consciousness allows you to tap into the divinity of the Father through your thoughts. Jesus said, "I can of mine own self [the mortal flesh] do nothing" (John 5:30). It is only when you bypass the natural and let love work through you that you "can do all things through Christ Jesus which strengtheneth" you (Philippians 4:13).

If we are aware of the Power of Love, we see its operation in us. The spiritual realm is hidden unless we are conscious of it—then we see the miraculous in operation. When we see the hand of God at work, we know God has empowered us to participate with Him.

How do you see the hand of God in operation? When do you feel your thoughts are empowered to do what otherwise would be impossible feats? How do you plan to strengthen your faith? If faith is the starting point of accumulated riches in the natural and spiritual, how would you rate your faith?

People who put up roadblocks to love are literally ruled by fear, but love rules in peace.

—ADAPTED FROM *THE PRAYER OF LOVE*

FOR YOUR THOUGHTS:

WEEK 4: STRENGTHENING CHARACTER

DAY 24: JUDGMENT

THINK AND DO

You are the person who has to decide whether
you'll do it or toss it aside; you are the person who makes
up your mind whether you'll lead or will linger behind.
Whether you'll try for the goal that's afar or just be
contented to stay where you are.

—EDGAR A. GUEST

IF WE WANT TO ACTIVATE the supernatural in our lives, it's simple: thoughts plus actions—think and do. Obviously this isn't something new. Some of us learned grammar by using a series called the Think and Do Workbooks.

This fundamental approach to learning (think and do) may be very similar to the spiritual application of faith shown by actions. It's first the natural, then the spiritual— we learn from the natural realm to understand the spiritual.

As children we began learning the structure and vocabulary of language with the objective to interpret our natural world—but what about the spiritual language? We may have managed to identify the spiritual "groanings" (Romans 8:26) Paul wrote about, but do we really understand the language and function of the Kingdom?

"For it is God who works in you both to will and to do for His good pleasure" (Philippians 2:13, NKJV). God energizes our thoughts with the ability to accomplish them. Our thoughts and actions together release the power of God—without this combination there is no life-activating power. Just as "faith without works is dead" (James 2:26, NKJV), so are thoughts without actions!

"Without faith it is impossible to please him" (Hebrews

11:6). If what you're doing is the plan of God for your life, then it becomes the outworking of His Kingdom on the earth.

The ability to make sound judgments—to know what is of God or not of God is important. You are the product of your thoughts and actions. One without

We learn from the natural realm to understand the spiritual.

the other is unproductive, or, as the apostle Paul called it, "the futility of [the] mind" (Ephesians 4:17, NKJV).

Are you a work in progress? How would you describe your faith proven by works? Do you work out your ideas? When you read a book, do you apply its message to your life? What do you do with inspiration?

There is a language of the spirit, and it's the communication of love. . . . There is a requirement that you learn the grammar and patterns of the language . . . and to be aware that you are a spiritual being in a natural body. You have the ability to know and hear God, which is the beginning of discernment.

—ADAPTED FROM *THE PRAYER OF LOVE*

FOR YOUR THOUGHTS:

GOOD ENOUGH

It is within my power either to serve God or not to serve Him. Serving Him, I add to my own good and the good of the whole world. Not serving Him, I forfeit my own good and deprive the world of that good, which was in my power to create.

—LEO TOLSTOY

MANY CHRISTIANS ARE IN SELF-HELP mode—they want to correct what's wrong with them. This started back in the Garden of Eden. "God saw every thing that he had made, and, behold, it was very good" (Genesis 1:31). God approved the excellence of his work. He made man in His image. Yet Adam and Eve didn't think they were good enough, so they yielded to the temptation to improve themselves.

Not knowing the truth, we work against His plan for us.

Eating from the fruit of the tree of the knowledge of good and evil was supposed to make them feel "good enough." But it changed their perception to shame. Now they viewed everything from their lack and shortcomings. They fell short of the grace of God and made clothes to cover themselves—still ashamed, they hid.

God's response to Adam and Eve was to ask, "Who told you that you were naked?" (Genesis 3:11, NKJV). God was never offended by their innocence, but steps were taken to redeem man from the error of not being good enough.

If we think we're inadequate, it will hinder our success in every realm. The negative thought causes defeat. Not knowing the truth, we work against His plan for us.

We hear in the language of our perception that what we see is true and accurate. If we're correcting our failures and think the purpose of our lives is to change what's wrong with us, then we'll never hear words about our strengths or what's good and excellent about us. The journey of self-improvement makes us self-conscious instead of God-conscious.

Do you focus more on what God thinks of you than what others think of you? Do you tend to work on perfecting areas you consider not good enough? Do you see yourself as made in God's image—think about who He is more than what you are not?

If our motive to change is to achieve happiness or position, it will produce limited benefit. This is why self-help techniques are always at a loss to bring lasting and life-altering change. If, however, our motive is love, then the power of God, who is Love, brings the change almost effortlessly.

—ADAPTED FROM *THE PRAYER OF LOVE*

FOR YOUR THOUGHTS:

WEEK 4: STRENGTHENING CHARACTER

DAY 26: SINCERITY

CREATING ATMOSPHERE

---

*If you sustain an atmosphere long enough,
you create a climate for things to grow. If you prolong a
climate to a growing season, you establish an environment.
If you maintain your environment to endure seasonal
changes, you create your own culture. Over time the
language, government, and culture of the area
become uniquely your own.*

—MARK HANBY

OUR THOUGHTS CREATE A HOLDING pattern in the atmosphere around us. How we think or feel controls whether we're bumping into destructive storm clouds that hold us back or enjoying the sunshine of wide-open spaces that illuminate a brighter future.

If you feel disappointed or frustrated that your life didn't turn out the way you wanted, you can still change it. Just as a pianist can choose to strike a different key or a dancer can learn a new step, you can choose to move in another direction. Creative thoughts charge the atmosphere with possibility—every time you bump into one of these thoughts, you feel empowered.

> *If you feel disappointed or frustrated that your life didn't turn out the way you wanted, you can still change it.*

One way to be more sincere in our daily lives is to consider how we think—two opposing thoughts cannot co-exist. We can know how we think by the way we feel.

- Positive thoughts: *creative* thought-patterns motivate, rejuvenate, and heal.
- Negative thoughts: *destructive* thought-patterns depress, discourage, and destroy.

David R. Hawkins believed that like the sun, the inner self is always shining, but because of negative clouds, we may not experience the warmth. However, if we remove the clouds—the willingness to let go of the habits of negative thinking—we can experience positive energy fields. "The removal of the obstacles to experience this," Hawkins said, "will result in an increasing sense of aliveness and a joy of one's own existence."

It's your choice. Do you want to step into an energized field of creative power? You can call to mind "whatsoever things are pure . . . lovely . . . of good report; . . . think on these things" (Philippians 4:8). Merely holding good thoughts in your mind attracts more good thoughts, and eventually the atmosphere around you reflects character that is sincerely rooted in love.

What kind of atmosphere do you create? Are you in a holding pattern? What do you think about? Are you happy with your life the way it is?

You can refuse to change the way you think and remain living in your problems, or you can choose better thoughts and live the good life. Either way, it remains your choice. So if you don't like your life, change it.

—ADAPTED FROM *THE PRAYER OF LOVE*

FOR YOUR THOUGHTS:

WEEK 4: STRENGTHENING CHARACTER

DAY 27: WITHOUT OFFENSE

OUR TRUE NATURE

---

*God is more concerned about our character than
our comfort. His goal is not to pamper us physically
but to perfect us spiritually.*

—PAUL W. POWELL

*Then [Joseph] lifted his eyes and saw his brother Benjamin,
his mother's son, and said, "Is this your younger brother of
whom you spoke to me?" And he said, "God be gracious
to you, my son." Now his heart yearned for his brother;
so Joseph made haste and sought somewhere to weep.
And he went into his chamber and wept there.*

—GENESIS 43:29–30, NKJV

YOUR TRUE NATURE IS APPARENT when things don't go the way you plan. It's that moment of response that tells it all—lets everyone else know the level of your maturity.

You may think you hold no offense, but when you are slighted, you react. God is fashioning you into His Image. You are "works in progress." What happens to you is for your perfection. It's all part of preparing you to fulfill your destiny.

In the biblical account of Joseph we see his split-second response to meeting his brothers. He didn't punish his brothers at their first encounter but arranged to see his younger brother.

Meeting Benjamin deeply touched Joseph and stirred up memories of home. Joseph had been in Egypt for more years than Benjamin had been alive. Seeing his mother's only other son seemed to make him homesick. But he blessed Benjamin in the tender words of a father—wishing his brother the best.

You may think you hold no offense but when you are slighted, you react.

There was no bitterness in Joseph over the cruelty of his brothers—he loved them. He was glad to be in Egypt, believing it was ordained by God to keep his family alive during the famine. Isn't it moving to see a world leader with a heart of compassion?

How do you react when things don't go your way? Do you forgive and love those who are cruel or inconsiderate to you? If God uses circumstances in our lives to mold godly character, what is He forming in you? How are your circumstances a necessary benchmark in your maturity?

You will never deal with any issue of offense before you first decide that you want to follow after love in that situation. You can have no release from the crippling effects of your offense before you choose to seek love.

—ADAPTED FROM *THE PRAYER OF LOVE*

FOR YOUR THOUGHTS:

WEEK 4: STRENGTHENING CHARACTER

DAY 28: FRUITS OF RIGHTEOUSNESS

EMPOWERED TO DO
WHAT'S RIGHT

But he who practices truth [who does what is right]
comes out into the Light; so that his works may be
plainly shown to be what they are—wrought with
God [divinely prompted, done with God's
help, in dependence upon Him].

—JOHN 3:21, AMP

THE FRUITS OF THE SPIRIT empower us to do what's right . . . but do we think that means just to stop a speeding bullet or to defy gravity? Superman had power, and so do we! But our power comes from the air we breathe—God's Breath of Life and His Spirit fill us with the ability to do all things in Him—the ability to strengthen our character.

Every moment of every day can be a breath of fresh air—of spiritual empowerment.

Jesus came to set things right, to undo all that the curse and our fears created. We don't have to be afraid of failing or making a mistake, of meeting new people, driving on the freeway, walking into new situations—the list is endless, but so is His Grace of Empowerment.

If He came "that [we] might have life, and that [we] might have it more abundantly" (John 10:10), then His Breath empowers everything we do—including all our responsibilities.

Doing the right thing—out of a godly character—includes providing an income and maintaining a household, raising a family and caring for the elderly, extending the hand of friendship and making things easier for others. It's a whole host of everyday actions we take because we want to live a rich life and enrich life for the people around us. In the process of our living in the Light, the Hand of God is manifested in our lives.

Every moment of every day can be a breath of fresh air—of spiritual empowerment. When things get tough or frightening, remember whose Breath you breathe. If you change your thoughts and habits to His thoughts and ways, then you are empowered from on high to do the impossible. You are more than Superman or Wonder Woman—you are a new person in Christ!

Even in your distress you can hold on to the hand that strengthens you and become a Light that shines brightly for the world to see. It's His perfect love in you that casts out fear.

What are your fears? How would Jesus speak to your fear? What can you do today that would right an area of responsibility you've neglected? What can you do to improve life for someone else?

The right way is the God way, or the spiritual way. The wrong way is the carnal way—not originating in the spirit but in our fleshly thoughts and desires.

—ADAPTED FROM *THE PRAYER OF LOVE*

FOR YOUR THOUGHTS:

WEEK 5: OPERATING IN THE SUPERNATURAL

DAY 29: ABOUNDING LOVE

PROSPER IN ALL THINGS

Beloved, I wish above all things that thou mayest prosper and be in health, even as thy soul prospereth. For I rejoiced greatly, when the brethren came and testified of the truth that is in thee, even as thou walkest in the truth. I have no greater joy than to hear that my children walk in truth.

—3 JOHN 1:2–4

To "PROSPER" MEANS THAT YOU advance or increase mentally, spiritually, emotionally, and physically.

The apostle John wrote in his third epistle of the measure of truth in his friend Gaius—that he "walked the talk," and the news gave John tremendous joy. He wanted Gaius to remember that if he would "walk in the truth," then he'd prosper in everything—John specifically singled out his health. John knew, two millennium before science ever developed a means of measuring human energy, that positive thoughts increase man's vitality and energy field.

How you walk in truth affects your health. Negative emotions such as anger or fear literally change your heart rate, which not only disturbs your well-being but distresses the heart and blood vessels, sometimes to the extent of causing physical deterioration.

You can sometimes reverse the damaging effects with positive emotions such as love or gratitude. You actually feel their effect in operation when you send out loving thoughts. A simple act of generating love toward people or even pets will calm your heart rate.

If you're at peace, your whole body often functions in balanced harmony, and pulsates in the frequency of God's heartbeat. The same ebb and flow of life that vibrates in the intricate symphony of the universe finds expression in us, and its vibration is our distinct energy field—giving us optimal health, wellness, and unique creative expression.

How you walk in truth affects your health.

Next time you feel stress, think about a loved one and lift up a prayer of gratitude to God—and feel your love and appreciation well up within. Send an encouraging note expressing your love and gratitude, as did the apostle John.

Love seeks harmony. Love seeks to harmonize. The truth is that love is a universe: uni-verse—one verse, one song of harmony, and the harmony is really the love of God. We learn to sing the same song.

—ADAPTED FROM *THE PRAYER OF LOVE*

FOR YOUR THOUGHTS:

WHEN GOD SPEAKS

God did not write a book and send it by messenger to be read at a distance by unaided minds. He spoke a Book and lives in His spoken words, constantly speaking His words and causing the power of them to persist across the years.

—A. W. TOZER

Making your ear attentive to skillful and godly Wisdom and inclining and directing your heart and mind to understanding [applying all your powers to the quest for it]; . . . For the Lord gives skillful and godly Wisdom; from His mouth come knowledge and understanding.

—PROVERBS 2:2, 6, AMP

SOMETHING ALWAYS HAPPENS when God speaks. Every word has purpose; He spoke His creation into existence. That would make hearing what He speaks very significant.

The promise in Proverbs says that if we seek and recognize His Word as wisdom, we'll receive the rich outpouring of His knowledge and understanding. God is the source of all wisdom.

Studying God's Word allows you to learn what God thinks.

The British philosopher Alfred North Whitehead said, "In a sense, knowledge shrinks as wisdom grows: for details are swallowed up in principles. The details of knowledge which are important will be picked up ad hoc in each avocation of life, but the habit of the active utilization of well-understood principles is the final possession of wisdom."

God spoke to Israel through the prophets. He still speaks to us. The written Word retains God's power—His Word cannot return void. It remains just as potent today as the moment He spoke it.

Studying God's Word allows you to learn what God thinks. The key to its effectiveness or power rests on whether you *apply* what you understand. If you practice what you understand from God, then discernment and good judgment further develop in your life.

How does God speak to you? Are there things you can do to make your ears more attentive? What does God speak to you? How can you apply it to your life?

Divine whisperings are God's wisdom continually spoken to each of us if we are sensitive enough to listen.

—ADAPTED FROM *THE PRAYER OF LOVE*

FOR YOUR THOUGHTS:

COMMANDING POWER

---

*I am crucified with Christ: nevertheless I live;
yet not I, but Christ liveth in me: and the life which I now
live in the flesh I live by the faith of the Son of God,
who loved me, and gave himself for me. I do not frustrate
the grace of God: for if righteousness come by the law,
then Christ is dead in vain.*

—GALATIANS 2:20–21

FREEDOM IS THE STATE OF MIND that enables you to act and live as you choose without being subject to any undue restraints or restrictions. Jesus released you from your personal prison, which confined you to an unproductive way of life. He determined to obey His Father—paying the ultimate price for your freedom.

Why grapple in our own efforts to stay alive when we can be empowered by the grace (anointing) of God? Death has no power over us—we are free! What we call failure is not falling down, but staying down.

Your faith opens the door to the rich outpouring of God.

Remember that Jesus died instead of you—it means you now live as Christ! Nothing can stop you from fulfilling your purpose. The curtain rent at His death symbolized that you now have access to the Fullness of God. Your faith opens the door to the full outpouring of God.

You are the temple of God. If you neglect this Truth, you'll continually frustrate your purpose by failing to access the grace available to you in the Body of Christ. Jesus' death gave access to the fullness of God. Jesus said, "If ye abide in me, and my words abide in you, ye shall ask what ye will, and it shall be done unto you" (John 15:7). God's

Word has *commanding power*. When we learn how to judge what is of God's leading, then we're ready to take the next step to operate in the supernatural.

Does God's Word have commanding power in your life? Are you free? Do you judge yourself worthy to receive God's grace? What hinders you from fulfilling your purpose?

Since love is living, it has power to grow and to eventually displace anything that is contrary to it. Knowledge and judgment are the fertile fields into which love is sown, and from which appears a multiplying harvest of its precious and sought-after fruit.

—ADAPTED FROM *THE PRAYER OF LOVE*

FOR YOUR THOUGHTS:

WEEK 5: OPERATING IN THE SUPERNATURAL

DAY 32: APPROVING EXCELLENCE

THE POWER OF BELIEF

---

*Trust thyself: every heart vibrates to
that iron string. . . . Great men have always done
so . . . betraying their perception that the absolutely
trustworthy was seated at their heart, working through
their hands, predominating in all their being.*

—RALPH WALDO EMERSON

GOD DWELLS WITHIN YOU. Emerson refers to Him as "the absolutely trustworthy . . . seated [in your] heart." God is the invisible power working through your hands. If you approve the excellence of the Presence of His Power dwelling within you, you'll be confident in what you do. Self-confidence is simply the manifestation of a heart that trusts in God.

"'For I know the plans I have for you,' declares the LORD, 'plans to prosper you and not to harm you, plans to give you hope and a future'" (Jeremiah 29:11, NIV). Do you believe God? Believing means you're receiving. If you feel His promise is too good for you, or that it's contingent on what you do, you're not receiving it.

Jesus said, "Signs shall follow them that believe" (Mark 16:17). First we believe and then what we believe is confirmed with substance. It's that simple. The believing puts us in the pathway to receive. We believe it's possible and it is—we expect it to happen and it does.

> Self-confidence is simply the manifestation of a heart that trusts in God.

"The testimony of Jesus is the spirit of prophecy" (Revelation 19:10). There's unlimited power available for those who believe the declaration of Jesus. The real essence of His power rests in what we believe. Let God's love saturate your heart and soul. Be confident that His power is in you and you will witness the unfolding of the miraculous.

"He who comes from heaven is above all. And what He has seen and heard, that He testifies; . . . He who has received His testimony has certified that God is true" (John 3:31–33, NKJV). A testimony is the evidence or record of what you witnessed God do! What do you see God doing? You are the testimony of what He's done through you— how He upholds your belief in Him.

Are you confident that God will supply your needs? When was the last time God showed you what He wanted you to do? How did you trust that it would happen? What can you do to tap into more of God?

Abounding love is when you are willing to take the individual emotions and attitudes (good and bad) and situations (pleasant or troublesome) and allow them, regardless of their nature, to increase your love.

—ADAPTED FROM *THE PRAYER OF LOVE*

FOR YOUR THOUGHTS:

WEEK 5: OPERATING IN THE SUPERNATURAL

DAY 33: SINCERITY

MEN OF STRONG PASSION

---

*When the hour had come, He sat down, and
the twelve apostles with Him. Then He said to them,
"With fervent desire I have desired to eat this
Passover with you before I suffer."*

—LUKE 22:14–15, NKJV

JESUS LONGED TO BE WITH His disciples on the feast of the Passover because He desired to explain to them His passion—everything that would happen to fulfill His purpose. There's always a cost to fulfilling our purpose.

Passion is defined as "a strong emotion, an art of love; zeal; eager desire; hope and joy." The author of Hebrews tells us, "For the joy that was set before him [He] endured the cross" (12:2). "With fervent desire" meant Jesus had zeal to fulfill His purpose—He felt the rush of adrenaline. He knew He was on earth to make a difference. He wanted to make our lives better.

The fathers of our country were passionate believers in freedom, wanting a better world for their children to inherit. Their sincerity and singleness of purpose fueled a revolution. Did you ever notice that those who fulfill their purpose are also impassioned to give their all—to be the best they can be? The French revolutionary Honoré Gabriel Riqueti, comte de Mirabeau, aptly said, "None but people of strong passions are capable of rising to greatness."

Passion to fulfill a specific purpose means ordinary people like you and me accomplish extraordinary things.

Having a purpose and pursuing it fervently will give

meaning to your life. Alfred Lord Tennyson said, "The happiness of a man in his life does not consist in the absence but in the mastering of his passions." Passion to fulfill a specific purpose means ordinary people like you and me accomplish extraordinary things.

Everyone has a purpose for being alive. Life means something when you know what you're called to do. God empowers you to fulfill your destiny. The zeal or energy He gave you will cause frustration if you don't know what to do with it. But searching for ways to manifest your zeal will usher in the supernatural.

Do you know your purpose? When putting together your to-do list, what items give you a rush—an excitement to work on them? Is there something you'd like to do that would make life better for others? What stops you from doing it?

If you're in life for yourself, you can have human success, but spiritual success is built on being sincere with other people and most of all with yourself. Each person has a great destiny, but it can only come to pass in an atmosphere of sincerity.

—ADAPTED FROM *THE PRAYER OF LOVE*

FOR YOUR THOUGHTS:

SOME THINGS JUST HAPPEN

---

*But I want you to know, brethren, that the things which
happened to me have actually turned out for the
furtherance of the gospel, so that it has become
evident to the whole palace guard, and to all
the rest, that my chains are in Christ.*

—PHILIPPIANS 1:12–13, NKJV

THERE ARE TIMES IN LIFE when you don't know if you're in or out of the will of God. You may question whether you're being punished. Job felt that way in his affliction; he felt wrongfully accused by his friends and questioned where God was.

In Egypt the Israelites were promised a country—yet how many died in the wilderness? Those who lived still had to travel through the wilderness before they could claim the Promised Land—and had to fight battles before moving in. The Promised Land was there before them, but they couldn't enter in until they got through the wilderness.

Sometimes we compare those who are very blessed with those who are not so blessed, and we question the integrity or faith of the less blessed. God opened the prison for Peter, so why didn't He for Paul? It's difficult to comprehend God's intention.

The apostle Paul saw miraculous things happen in his ministry, yet he was confined to prison. He understood that the things that happened to him were for the "furtherance of the gospel" (Philippians 1:12)—to fulfill his destiny. He was content and held no offense toward God or man for what he endured.

What if the very thing you're struggling with is designed to be a doorway? What if the longing in your soul is actually meant to motivate you to step into another area of possibility? If you don't understand what's happening to you, that your "obstacle" may be part of the process, you may miss the opportunity within it.

What if the very thing you're struggling with is designed to be a doorway?

If you are open to what God says, it will shift your thoughts into the realm of understanding—not only to see the plan but to understand what must be done to make it happen. God knows your end from the beginning—that's what *plan* means.

Are the things that have happened to you part of your personal process and journey? Did you recognize a doorway in your struggle? Do you know God's plan for you?

We think the things we go through in life—the struggles with children, financial problems, or marital challenges—are there to harm us, but the truth is, if we have a mature attitude toward life, we understand that really these things are often the fire of God to show us our character flaws.

—ADAPTED FROM *THE PRAYER OF LOVE*

FOR YOUR THOUGHTS:

WEEK 5: OPERATING IN THE SUPERNATURAL

DAY 35: FRUITS OF RIGHTEOUSNESS

GLORY TO GLORY

When one turns to the Lord, the veil is taken away.
Now the Lord is the Spirit; and where the Spirit of
the Lord is, there is liberty. But we all, with unveiled face,
beholding as in a mirror the glory of the Lord, are being
transformed into the same image from glory to glory,
just as by the Spirit of the Lord.

—2 CORINTHIANS 3:16–18, NKJV

UNDER THE OLD COVENANT, the letter of the law punished with death. But under the New Covenant, the Spirit sets us free from the bondage of death. We experience liberty.

Mankind was doomed—but then the Spirit of Life set us free. As we conform to the image of Christ, He liberates us.

The veil is removed through Christ. *Christ* means "anointed." It's difficult to imagine, but we accept God's thoughts by the simple act of believing that His Word is for us.

We have glorious hope—joyful and confident expectation. We are free . . . totally receptive . . . and eternally liberated!

How does this work? All of us are enabled to receive through the abounding love of God's anointing. If we accept it, then His Word forms in us.

All of us are enabled to receive through the abounding love of God's anointing.

That means we mirror what we see and hear by what we believe. And because we're agreeable, we are constantly being transformed into His very own image! We evolve into Divine Form as His Word becomes flesh in us!

Our thoughts are being changed into His thoughts—His Divine Form abides within us and manifests as fruits of righteousness.

How do you manifest the fruits of righteousness? Is there something you see as divine that you emulate? How do people say you are Christ-like? Is it revealed in mercy . . . love . . . kindness . . . encouragement . . . resourcefulness?

As you are filled with the fruits of righteousness, thinking and acting as God does, you appropriate His victory over sin. You become transformed by "The Prayer of Love" into the image of God by taking on His nature.

—ADAPTED FROM *THE PRAYER OF LOVE*

FOR YOUR THOUGHTS:

SUCH A TIME AS THIS

---

*Nothing can withstand the power of the
human will if it is willing to stake its very existence
to the extent of its purpose.*

—BENJAMIN DISRAELI

*Events of history have not happened by chance but by
God's choice to fulfill His plan for the nations. One's
personal destiny is part of God's overall plan, and
what happens in the lives of individuals often has
great effect on the course of history.*

—STEPHEN MCDOWELL

IN THE FIFTH CENTURY BC, Scripture records that Esther became like a daughter to her uncle Mordecai after her parents died. She was taken along with many beautiful young virgins into the citadel to be considered by King Ahasuerus to replace Queen Vashti.

Esther was chosen to be queen—her life relegated to confinement if she didn't. She was a Jew but didn't reveal her identity to the king because her uncle Mordecai advised against it. Then a decree was sent throughout the kingdom to annihilate all Jews, and Mordecai asked Esther to share her secret with her husband, the king. Perhaps he would have mercy on all Jews because of his love for Esther.

Have you ever sacrificed to save someone else?

Esther was reluctant to obey her uncle for two good reasons. First, she replaced a queen who didn't follow protocol—and that queen was banished for her insubordination. Second, the law stated that if she approached the king without being summoned, he could put her to death. And the king hadn't asked for Esther for a month.

Mordecai reminded Esther that if she didn't speak for the Jews, he would perish along with his family—and she was his family. Mordecai ended his request with a statement that seemed to highlight Esther's destiny: "Who knoweth whether thou art come to the kingdom for such a time as this?" (Esther 4:14).

Divine intervention made Esther queen, to play a key part in Israel's history. It took courage for her to approach the king, but she trusted God would work through her to save the Jews. Esther faced death saying, "So will I go in unto the king, which is not according to the law: and if I perish, I perish" (Esther 4:16).

She was willing to lay down her life if it meant saving the Jews. Have you ever sacrificed to save someone else? You show abounding love when you sacrifice for the cause of freedom . . . or donate a kidney . . . or yield your will that God's may be done.

Love lays down its life. Love gives, fear withholds. Love surrenders, fear threatens. If you truly love, then you are willing not just to give things, but to give yourself.

—ADAPTED FROM *THE PRAYER OF LOVE*

FOR YOUR THOUGHTS:

TRANSCENDING POWER

---

*I've never met a person, I don't care what his condition,
in whom I could not see possibilities. I don't care how
much a man may consider himself a failure, I believe in
him, for he can change the thing that is wrong in his life
anytime he is prepared and ready to do it. Whenever he
develops the desire, he can take away from his life
the thing that is defeating it. The capacity for
reformation and change lies within.*

—PRESTON BRADLEY

THERE'S TRANSCENDING POWER IN God's Word. By thinking godly thoughts, you can escape the natural, material world of failure to experience the eternal realm of limitless power and possibility in the supernatural. The author and motivational teacher Napoleon Hill said, "The majority of men meet with failure because of their lack of persistence in creating new plans to take the place of those which fail."

Knowing truth is the transcending power that sets our minds free to take the risk toward success.

The apostle Paul wrote to Timothy, advising him to be a leader "in humility correcting those who are in opposition, if God perhaps will grant them repentance, so that they may know the truth" (2 Timothy 2:25, NKJV). At the time, the Greeks considered "repentance" (*metanoia*) to be a transcendence of the mind: *meta*—"above, beyond" and *noia*—"of mind." If we grasp this definition, we comprehend the deeper meaning of learning—"that they may know the truth."

Learning involves a fundamental shift. It's the progressive movement of the mind. Learning is more than taking in information; it generates your ability to create. It's the essence of creative expression that transcends information and connects you to the supernatural.

The medical doctor and author Maxwell Maltz said, "Often the difference between a successful man and a failure is not one's better abilities or ideas, but the courage that one has to bet on his ideas, to take the calculated risk and to act." Knowing truth is the transcending power that sets your mind free to take the risk toward success. You're on a journey to know the deep things of God—a journey of love.

Have you experienced the transcending power of God's Word? How has it impacted your life? Did you experience something supernatural? What did you learn?

Knowledge by itself can never bring change to struggles that lie deep within the human spirit. Instead, these changes come by love through spiritual maturity. Learning to pray, "Let my love abound in all knowledge," opens the process of divine knowledge that is able to bring a spiritual alteration by allowing love to grow beyond human limitation.

—ADAPTED FROM *THE PRAYER OF LOVE*

FOR YOUR THOUGHTS:

WEEK 6: LIVING YOUR IDEALS

DAY 38: JUDGMENT

STRENGTH UNDER CONTROL

---

*In the Greek "prautes" [meekness] basically is connected
with anger. . . . [It] is the quality of the man who is
angry for the right reasons, against the right people,
in the right way, and for the right length of time.
The basic idea of the word is not so much
gentleness as strength under control.*

—WILLIAM BARCLAY

MEEKNESS IS A VIRTUE. If we dislike who we are—hate the sound of our voice, despise our physical features, wish we were as talented or successful as someone else—then we are not meek.

The meek learn to accept everything about themselves as part of their eternal makeup. They learn to be satisfied with who they are because they are made in God's image for a specific purpose only they can fulfill.

Meek has often been used to describe wild horses. It refers to an inner will or energy willing to be guided and directed. The horses' strength is harnessed. Likewise a disciple is trained or meek if his self-will has been brought to judgment—he judges himself. It's the love of God that changes us.

Inner strength and courage are outwardly portrayed as meekness or gentleness. Jesus said, "Come unto me, all ye that labour and are heavy laden, and I will give you rest. Take my yoke upon you, and learn of me; for I am meek and lowly in heart: and ye shall find rest unto your souls" (Matthew 11:28–29).

God will never harm or hurt us; He loves us. The time Moses angrily hit the rock to bring forth water—rather than speak to it as God commanded—cost him entry into the Promised Land (Numbers 20:1–13). Moses' action was contrary to God's holiness. We can judge ourselves: If we hurt ourselves or others with our anger, we are not meek. If we lose our temper, we are not meek. Meekness is not a behavior; it is who we are all the time.

Do you have the right kind of temper—a righteous anger? What happens when this is stirred up in you? Are you in control of your life—yielded to God? Do you know your limits and accept them? Would you consider yourself to be meek? Whom do you see as meek—why?

Inner strength and courage are outwardly portrayed as meekness or gentleness.

Judgment is the ability to make good choices in life, because you realize you're part of God's universe, part of a greater plan. You know who you are, so you are not ashamed of yourself. Your actions and attitudes submitted to judgment will bring forth responsibility.

—ADAPTED FROM *THE PRAYER OF LOVE*

FOR YOUR THOUGHTS:

WEEK 6: LIVING YOUR IDEALS

DAY 39: APPROVING EXCELLENCE

IN GOD WE TRUST

Praise the Power that hath made and preserved us a nation.
Then conquer we must, when our cause it is just, and this
be our motto: "In God is our trust."

—FRANCIS SCOTT KEY

OUR NATIONAL ANTHEM CITES AMERICA as the "land of the free and the home of the brave." We desire to build on what's true, honorable, right, and just, expanding on the original tenets of our beliefs as a nation formed under God.

We love liberty. We look to those who stood in the gap in the past, such as the apostles Paul and Peter, William Wallace, Joan of Arc, Martin Luther, George Washington, John Adams, Thomas Jefferson, Abraham Lincoln, William Wilberforce, Dr. Martin Luther King, and Nelson Mandela—but who will stand in the gap now?

One generation gave their lives and their fortunes to ensure our future by founding a nation that destined liberty for *all*. And yet, if that liberty is withheld from some, then that nation cannot stand under its founding truth because it has lost its purpose. Abraham

Who will stand in the gap now?

Lincoln's primary concern for commemorating a portion of a battlefield at Gettysburg for future generations was for remembering the eternal truths—the basic principles of liberty. Sensing the enormity of the crisis that lay before the nation, he made a decision to ensure liberty for *all* people. The men did not die in vain if the founding principles were upheld.

Lincoln advanced freedom for the unity of the brotherhood. He fought for justice and peace through the manifestation of love in our nation and abroad. Dr. Martin Luther King, Jr., picked up the chords of "a battle cry for freedom" and while advocating nonviolence sang, "We shall overcome." Through his unwavering efforts, our nation passed the Civil Rights Act in 1964.

What will you stamp on our age? Will you leave behind some worthy cause that others will build upon? It's time to reevaluate your beliefs so that you know what you'll fight for—what really makes a difference. What would you spend the rest of your life pursuing because you are devoted to that higher ideal—a desire for greater excellence?

In approving excellence, you seek to find not only the good but also what is better.

—ADAPTED FROM *THE PRAYER OF LOVE*

FOR YOUR THOUGHTS:

Cellular Memory

---

*The character that takes command in moments of crucial
choices has already been determined by a thousand other
choices made earlier in seemingly unimportant moments. It
has been determined by all the "little" choices of years
past—by all those times when the voice of conscience was
at war with the voice of temptation . . . whispering the lie
that "it really doesn't matter." It has been determined by all
the day-to-day decisions made when life seemed easy and
crisis seemed far away—the decisions that, piece by piece,
bit by bit, developed habits of discipline or of laziness;
habits of self-sacrifice or self-indulgence; habits of duty and
honor and integrity—or dishonor and shame.*

—RONALD REAGAN

GOD IS LOVE. THE WAY you develop more love (more spiritual power and energy) is by choosing to keep His commandment to love Him with your all.

Love is the greatest commandment—it changes every dimension of our lives. Whoever believes God and keeps His commandments chooses life. Choosing life or death begins with our everyday decisions. Our choices characterize the level of our sincerity.

The difference between life and death is in your choice of response—your heart chooses to love God or not. The more you practice doing right, the more you reinforce the pathways of virtue that support a strong character link to God.

The Bible records God's story of interaction with His creation. Nature has a memory also. Trees maintain a history in their rings . . . the earth's strata reveals the history of catastrophes—the Flood, the Ice Age, volcanoes, and so on.

The natural body also has cellular memory that retains our health history. But illness can be a law written in our cells that keeps our body captive. The cure-all is the re- generating power of the Holy Spirit and meditation—a hands-on spiritual therapy for removing any lingering addictions, including the deep and hidden damage of the "old nature."

The higher energy of His Love overpowers the damaging lower frequencies. His high vibrating power sets us free—"the law of the Spirit of life in Christ Jesus hath made me free from the law of sin and death" (Romans 8:2).

The residual effects of stress and anxiety need to be continually eliminated from our bodies. "He sent his word, and healed them, and delivered them from their destructions" (Psalm 107:20). If His Word resonates in you, then the same power finds a connection in you and can restore your heart, body, mind, and strength. If He chooses, He can miraculously rewrite the cellular memory of your DNA.

> *The difference between life and death is in your choice of response—your heart chooses to love God or not.*

It's not so much what you think but how you think that determines your character.

—ADAPTED FROM *THE PRAYER OF LOVE*

FOR YOUR THOUGHTS:

THE REAL CHAMPIONS

*You are what you repeatedly do. Excellence is
not an event—it is a habit.*

—ARISTOTLE

SOMEONE ONCE SAID, "Most look up and admire the stars. A champion climbs a mountain and grabs one."

It's never enough to admire the stars or esteem the ideals of other great men and women; we must make our own goals. Those who do are the real champions.

Challenges become the stepping-stones to achieving goals. Three hundred men blew their trumpets, declaring, "The sword of the Lord, and of Gideon!" and walked over the walls to capture the stronghold at Jericho (Judges 7). Joab's small band of men climbed up an underground water shaft to defeat the Jebusites and take the stronghold at Jerusalem for David (2 Samuel 5).

Feedback monitors our blind spots—letting us know whether we're on course or in need of adjustment.

Champions do great exploits. In 1987 Ronald Reagan didn't care if he offended someone when he gave a speech before the closed Brandenburg Gate in West Germany, saying, "Mr. Gorbachev, tear down this wall!" He championed freedom—and four years later the Berliners tore down the wall.

Thomas Edison relied on what didn't work to help him

succeed. When asked about his results, he replied, "If I found ten thousand ways something won't work, I haven't failed. I am not discouraged because every wrong attempt discarded is another step forward." Edison used feedback to narrow his options until he found the one filament that worked in a lightbulb.

Feedback monitors our blind spots—letting us know whether we're on course or in need of adjustment. Sincere input from others viewing our performance comes in the form of comments, opinions, or reactions to help us be more effective. Champions incorporate these recommendations immediately. If we're willing to accept constructive criticism and not be offended, we'll continually improve. Feedback is an opportunity to learn what works or doesn't work.

A champion is not annoyed by feedback. He knows it's never a personal attack on him—it's meant to improve his performance levels. Even if it sounds critical or negative, he'll consider it constructive because he desires to be better—and he'll become great.

How do you respond to negative feedback? What can you do to use it to your advantage? Whom do you esteem for their ideals? Why?

Mahatma Gandhi went on a hunger strike—believing the force of love would quell the violence.

—ADAPTED FROM *THE PRAYER OF LOVE*

FOR YOUR THOUGHTS:

WALL OF LIBERTY

Those from among you shall build the old waste places;
you shall raise up the foundations of many generations; and
you shall be called the Repairer of the Breach,
the Restorer of Streets to Dwell In.

—ISAIAH 58:12, NKJV

T HE HALL OF FAITH in the book of Hebrews is an example of a platform in the House of God. It records testimonies of those who fought the battle before us to make up the platform—a wall that bridged a breach.

June 6, 1944—now remembered as D-day in World War II—is a vivid portrayal of building a platform. The amphibious landing craft escorted around 156,000 assault forces to five beaches along the Normandy Coast. The enemy's formidable defenses on Omaha Beach included thirteen strongholds, and the water and beach were heavily mined. American casualties rose to almost 2,400 on that beach alone.

Many young men stepped off the landing craft and into watery graves. Some found their gear was too heavy to maneuver in the deep water. Many were gunned down by enemy fire. They heroically faced death. They chose to take the step even if it meant giving up their lives to build a platform of liberty.

Following Israel's victory during the 1967 Six-Day War, the Western Wall—also known as the Wailing Wall—came under Israeli control. Israel's fifth prime minister, Yitzhak Rabin, described the feeling in his Jerusalem Day Address to Knesset on May 29, 1995:

"There was one moment in the Six-Day War which symbolized the great victory: that was the moment in which the first paratroopers . . . reached the stones of the [Wailing Wall and felt] the emotion of the place; there never was, and never will be, another moment like it. Nobody staged that moment. . . . It was as if Providence had directed the whole thing: the paratroopers weeping loudly and in pain over their comrades who had fallen along the way, the words of the Kaddish prayer . . . after 19 years of silence, tears of mourning, shouts of joy, and the singing of 'Hatikvah.'"

How has your faith encouraged another to stand in difficult times?

In 1996 the Vietnam Veterans Memorial Wall was erected. Silence and mourning, respect and appreciation extend from those who place their hands upon the names of fallen family members or comrades. Since then, two replicas of the wall tour the United States each year— The Moving Wall and The Wall That Heals. These have become our wailing walls to remember the brave military men and women who put their lives on the line for freedom—they loved their country. Their lives give evidence of their fruit of righteousness in operation.

How have you become a platform for others to reach their purpose? How has your faith encouraged another to stand in difficult times?

The unmasking of the true inner spirit is continually seen in lives willing to love.

—ADAPTED FROM *THE PRAYER OF LOVE*

FOR YOUR THOUGHTS:

REINFORCING
HABITS

❧

SEVEN DAYS

LOVE IS WHAT LOVE DOES

---

*There is something of the essence of creative expression that
informs and transcends all its manifestations—and
when you touch it—magic!*

—ANNIE BEVAN

WHATEVER IS IN US is our essence—we cannot release love unless it's in us. William Shakespeare said, "They do not love who do not show their love." We can recognize people who love. An upbeat heart activates an energy field around the person, creating an air of encouragement or cooperation that others can actually feel.

If you lack love, the pervading air feels more like disagreeableness or unhelpfulness. The oppression can be stifling. But when your heart is harmonious with the Spirit, you profit and benefit physically, spiritually, and vocationally—you allow His love to balance you in every area of your life.

If your heart is determined, it motivates change and you will be able to break through damaging habits to prosper.

It's not surprising, then, that those who determine to love the Lord with all their hearts change from the inside out. Love causes the greatest transformation in us. If loving God becomes your motivation, it will initiate a change in your reactions, responses, and attitudes.

Our neural pathways are strengthened by use. The continual repetition of a certain response to an emotion creates a strong link or habit, and we do it without even thinking—much like operating on autopilot.

Once the pathway is habitually strengthened through constant use, it is nearly impossible to break. This is why addictions are so difficult—they're practiced without conscious thought. We can try to discipline ourselves, but this effort is effective only if we're determined to put our whole hearts into changing how we behave—half a heart won't work.

Your level of awareness increases in direct proportion to the amount of heart you put into what you do. If your heart is determined, it motivates change and you will be able to break through damaging habits to prosper. Soon you'll find the essence of your being exuberantly living life to the fullest. Your habitual lifestyle experiences a breakthrough, and you become who you always wanted to be.

You cannot change your behavior unless you change your habits. What habits are you changing? What is the expression of your love?

We all gravitate toward people who demonstrate compassion and genuine concern, and we tend to avoid those who are self-

serving and self-absorbed. Loving actions or attitudes contrary to love don't just happen but are a result of character.

—ADAPTED FROM *THE PRAYER OF LOVE*

FOR YOUR THOUGHTS:

RUN TO WIN

The high prize of life, the crowning fortune of a man, is to be born with a bias to some pursuit which finds him in employment and happiness—whether it be to make baskets, or broadswords, or canals, or statues, or songs.

—RALPH WALDO EMERSON

EMERSON SOUGHT TO FULFILL his dreams. He defined "the high prize of life" as "the crowning glory of a man." He understood that when we discover the meaning of our lives, what we do gives us tremendous satisfaction. Doing the work puts our thoughts into action. Eventually we reach our destiny.

"Without ambition," said Emerson, "one starts nothing. Without work one finishes nothing. The prize will not be sent to you. You have to win it." Ambition is a burning passion that sets the mind on fire. It energizes or fuels us with the knowledge of our purpose. Paul wrote that he didn't run a race with uncertainty—he ran to win the prize (Philippians 3:14). We win the prize also because we choose to do the work necessary to attain it.

Achievers are different from dreamers. You can dream about things being another way, but unless you implement a plan, nothing changes. Achievers have the ambition to work daily toward an end result. This is nothing new— Jesus spoke of those who hunger and thirst after righteousness. Like hunger, ambition is a daily drive—not a once-in-a-lifetime thought. Ambition empowers you to change.

Ambition is an inner vitality that pursues the prize of the upward call of God in our lives—it makes dreams happen. It's the determination that motivates us not only to seize the moment of transition but also to press into it for all its possibility.

Our goal or objective moves beyond the aspiration needed to make it happen. George Bernard Shaw said, "The people who get on in this world are the people who get up and look for the circumstances they want, and, if they can't find them, make them."

When we discover the meaning of our lives, what we do gives us tremendous satisfaction.

Endeavor to fuel a passion to move into deeper spiritual terrain by pursuing your high calling. What are your dreams? How are you ambitious to make your dreams happen? What kind of motivation keeps you targeted on the goal?

Knowledge by itself can never bring change to struggles that lie deep within the human spirit—these changes come by love through spiritual maturity.

—ADAPTED FROM *THE PRAYER OF LOVE*

FOR YOUR THOUGHTS:

TIMES THAT
TRY MEN'S SOULS

---

*The world is at this moment passing through one of
those terrible periods of convulsion when the souls of men
and of nations are tried as by fire. Woe to the man or to the
nation that at such a time stands as once Laodicea
stood; . . . when they dared not come to the help of the
Lord against the might. In such a crisis the moral weakling
is the enemy of the right, the enemy of life, liberty,
and the pursuit of happiness.*

—THEODORE ROOSEVELT

THERE WILL ALWAYS BE an overturning of events, a recurrent shifting until God's will is done. The physical creation groans without and the spiritual remnant groans within.

Any crisis can be emotionally difficult—but it has the potential to make us better. *Crisis* comes from the Greek word that means "decisive" or "point of decision." We come to a juncture and must decide which way we'll take.

What begins as a crisis moment may end as an opportunity that propels us further along our life journey—a supernatural "suddenly." Each crisis represents an opportunity to accomplish something linked to our ultimate purpose in God. It's important to know our purpose, or we may miss the opportunity each decision presents.

Each crisis represents an opportunity to accomplish something linked to our ultimate purpose in God.

A clear, specific decision empties our minds of doubt—it clears our minds to receive and allows us to freely tap into the supernatural. Many feel the love and peace of God even during times of chaos.

The crisis acts as a stimulus to release untapped powers if we focus on what we can do to make a difference. If we become conscious of the heightened energy that the crisis ignites in us, we can tap into it and harness it to overcome the situation. We don't even have to look for the next step—it will show up in a subsequent crisis.

There are moments in history when a portal opens and monumental change occurs. What if the events happening in our lives are hinged on recognizing these extraordinary moments? It's during "such a time as this" that you make your greatest contribution, because you discover the golden opportunity.

What type of trying situations have you endured? What decisions have you made? How would you describe a "portal moment" in history? How was it a turning point or an opportunity?

Judgment is simply the ability to make proper decisions.

—ADAPTED FROM *THE PRAYER OF LOVE*

FOR YOUR THOUGHTS:

HERE I AM

---

*Then flew one of the seraphims unto me, having a live coal
in his hand, which he had taken with the tongs from off the
altar: And he laid it upon my mouth, and said, Lo, this
hath touched thy lips; and thine iniquity is taken away, and
thy sin purged. Also I heard the voice of the Lord, saying:
Whom shall I send, and who will go for us?
Then I said, Here am I; send me.*

—ISAIAH 6:6–8

IN THE SCRIPTURE ABOVE Isaiah saw the Shekinah Glory (God's presence on earth) in the heavenly tabernacle of God and heard a voice that led to his opportunity in the supernatural. First he felt an unraveling of everything he deemed important—so much so that he felt unworthy of even being there. Then the angel of the Lord purged his mouth of all his doubtful, negative, destructive words and turned his testimony into a sacrifice of praise.

Never stop believing in Divine Intervention!

No longer did he think of why he couldn't do something or what was wrong with him—why God couldn't use him or why something couldn't be true. When he approved excellence, he thought differently, and everything changed—he was a new man.

Isaiah heard the voice of opportunity. Without hesitation he said, "Here am I! Send me." He believed he could do it. Isaiah knew the experience in the vision prepared him to speak and he was ready to do so.

Experience means you've been in similar situations before and learned valuable lessons. Along with experience comes the ability to stay calm—to trust in that inner sense that you recognize as God. You don't wait for someone else to step in because this is what you've been trained for—so you do your best. Some say their whole lives were training for those special moments.

Your inner knowledge of "I can do this" is another way of saying, "Here am I! Send me!" It's sensing and acting—believing that "I can do all things through Christ which strengtheneth me" (Philippians 4:13).

Never stop believing in Divine Intervention! Miracles happen! And if you're in a situation, consider how you can help—what you can offer. If you recognize the moment, you are able to walk in the synchronicity of unfolding events saying, "Here am I! Send me!" as you watch everything fall into place.

Great things happen when you commit yourself to do the work—Providence moves in extraordinary ways to bring it to pass. Has this ever happened to you? What do you see as a need? What can you do to help? What are you trained to do?

Things did not come about because of any wisdom or power on our part, but because we dared to see what would happen if we opened ourselves to the rule of love.

—ADAPTED FROM *THE PRAYER OF LOVE*

FOR YOUR THOUGHTS:

SYNCHRONICITY

We do not create our destiny; we participate in its
unfolding. Synchronicity works as a catalyst towards
the working out of that destiny.

—DAVID RICHO

AMERICANS APPLAUDED THE "miracle on the Hudson" in 2009. The commercial passenger flight incident was an incredible rescue. What could have been a horrendous airplane crash became instead an extraordinary splash.

Peter Greenberg (NBC News contributor) cited the amazing factors that came together for this spectacular landing and rescue. Experience was one: The pilot, Chesley Burnett "Sully" Sullenberger III was a former jet pilot who also operated a safety consulting firm. When a flock of birds disabled both engines, he managed to guide and safely land his Airbus on the Hudson River. Even the air traffic controller had twenty years of experience.

Nothing is truly random in this delicately ordered universe—including its seeming chaos.

Timing was also a key factor to the crew and passengers' success—food carts weren't in the way, passengers were still strapped in, and it was daylight. Weather was in their favor, too: no winds or waves. And location made a difference—the water landing meant many boats were close enough to help rescue passengers.

God's fingerprints were all over the success of that landing. So many things that could have gone wrong didn't, even when an attendant tried to open the back door of the plane and found it stuck. Peter Greenberg said, "This was actually fortunate, because if the door had opened, experts say the plane would have sunk fast. Instead what happened turned into part of the miracle: the flight attendant began ushering her passengers forward."

Synchronicity is the orchestration of events beyond our understanding or control. It's the combination of events unfolding together without any apparent underlying connection. Synchronicity is God working out everything for our good. All the pieces came together to accomplish a perfect landing. The testimony of the pilot's expertise further demonstrates his sincerity to improve air safety.

Regardless of how random events seem, there's always a reason for what happens. Nothing is truly random in this delicately ordered universe—including its seeming chaos. There's a rhyme and a reason to it, a Divine order that's always at work.

Has God orchestrated an event beyond your control that would have normally seemed impossible? Did you learn something about your sincerity or about yourself? Did it change the way you see God? How will you respond next time?

There comes a point as we mature that we begin to understand that eternal truths are infinite truths; that is, they are not limited to time or dimension.

—ADAPTED FROM *THE PRAYER OF LOVE*

FOR YOUR THOUGHTS:

———————

To the Mountaintop

———————

*[Dr. King had an] ultimate goal of healing and regenerating
an entire population . . . [to] eliminate injustice within
ourselves. . . . By reaching into and beyond ourselves and
tapping the transcendent moral ethic of love,
we shall overcome these evils.*

—CORETTA SCOTT KING

D R. MARTIN LUTHER KING, JR., had a dream that "with this faith we will be able to transform the jangling discords of our nation into a beautiful symphony of brotherhood . . . to sing together . . . Free at last! Free at last! Thank God Almighty, we are free at last!"

If only Dr. King had lived to see the fruit of his labors, he would have witnessed the freedom he had worked for rising to the next level of manifestation. He advocated a spiritual freedom from living without offense. He perceived the restoration of every man's rights as only the initial step toward freedom—the freedom to fulfill his responsibility.

Do we dare to believe that we can live by the Spirit, no longer ruled by the past but ruled only by His love?

Freedom is never about getting something for nothing—it's about getting what we want from life through use of our God-given abilities. Freedom is not remaining, or letting others remain, victims of poverty, hate, discrimination, injustice, or dysfunction; it is expressing His love and fulfilling our God-given responsibilities. As the heart is regenerated, mankind learns how to live in the spiritual kingdom; we lose our distinctions and become one in purpose. What the political system failed to finish in earlier centuries fell as a mantle on the man of God Dr. Martin Luther King, Jr.

We all share the same freedom. We can either use our freedom to fulfill our personal ambitions or plant our seed of purpose into another generation and work to eternally increase its productivity and measure. We actually take our knowledge of the Kingdom of God to a new level as freedom regenerates the Body of Christ.

America still mourns for Dr. King. He paid the ultimate price for freedom—he made a vital difference in our America.

Have we taken our liberty to the highest level of spirituality that Dr. King dreamed of? Do we dare to believe that we can live by the Spirit, no longer ruled by the past but ruled only by His love? What mantle has fallen to this generation . . . to you?

When we choose love, we become God's answer and take on the important mission of changing our world for good.

—ADAPTED FROM *THE PRAYER OF LOVE*

FOR YOUR THOUGHTS:

WEEK 7: TESTIMONIES OF A VICTORIOUS LIFE

DAY 49: FRUITS OF RIGHTEOUSNESS

———————

STAMP SOMETHING WORTHY

———————

*Every man should be ambitious to stamp something worthy
upon his age and leave behind him something which
the world will not willingly let die.*

—ORISON SWETT MARDEN

THOSE WHO'VE SPEARHEADED GREAT CAUSES live on in their testimonies. Martin Luther, John Knox, and John Calvin were part of a team of Reformers. But Calvin focused on collecting the important discover-ies of their day in order to record their history—their testimony. Rather than try to reinvent the wheel, he recognized what meth-ods of church and government were effective and kept an ac-count of them. He knew the re-corded material would be useful to the next generation, who could study and learn through their experience. He revered history as a record of what worked.

> *What have you experienced in life that would benefit another in his or her walk?*

John Calvin left his mark by writing books that not only documented the age he lived in but also became a blueprint for how church and government could be more effective.

Calvin started a work in progress in Geneva that tran-scended all types of known government in his day. It was the ministry of the saints governed by the people and for the people—something unheard of before Calvin's time.

He envisioned a better structure of government and wrote *The Institutes of Christian Religion*. Yet his vision wasn't fully implemented until a future generation came to America and used his writings to form a nation under God. It happened because Calvin created a practical application for spiritual truth—a platform for them to stand on.

America reveals the true ramifications of Calvin's ministry and the impact of his genius. The biographies of those who sought liberty had one common thread—they studied the works of John Calvin. Two hundred years after his death men and women were still reading his work, studying his form of government, and implementing his brilliance in the drafting of a constitution.

What is your testimony? What have you experienced in life that would benefit another in his or her walk? What can you do to increase your skill or expertise? Who could benefit from what you have learned? How can you pass on what you've experienced so your knowledge is not lost?

We need to encourage one another, but we also need to challenge one another. We can become better.

—ADAPTED FROM *THE PRAYER OF LOVE*

FOR YOUR THOUGHTS:

ACKNOWLEDGMENTS

Great devotionals are among the most unique of all literary compositions. Their basic purpose is not to inform, educate, or entertain but rather to inspire readers to open themselves to their inner and sometimes hidden emotions and motivations. In their ability to accomplish this task, they perform much the same as good poetry. Beyond this, devotionals give us a way, through the use of such devices as focused questioning and daily application, to take active steps to accomplish desired change. Therefore the mark of any successful devotional is not only that it exposes us to ourselves but that it actually brings forth desired change and increased connection with our distinctive spiritual nature.

We would like to acknowledge the contribution of Karen Roth in the development and writing of this devotional. Its authorship in many ways belongs to her. Most of the powerful techniques and insights in applying the principles found in *The Prayer of Love* come as a consequence of her dedication and spiritual experimentation. This devotional will bring forth transformational change because its tenets have been tested by time and formed in love. With much heartfelt love and appreciation, we thank you, Karen.